Pilotage

on

Inland Waterways

A Manual for Skippers and Crews of
Power Cruisers on Rivers and Canals

by

C. Cove-Smith and R. E. Chase

Published by
Yachting & Boating Weekly,
Illustrated Newspapers Ltd.,
Holborn Hall,
100 Gray's Inn Road,
London, W.C.1 8AP.

SBN 7207 0433 2
Distributed by
Pelham Books Ltd.,
52 Bedford Square,
London, W.C.1 1ES.

Printed by
Tonbridge Printers Ltd.,
Tonbridge,
Kent.

About the Authors

C. COVE-SMITH

is Honorary Assistant Secretary (Publicity) of the National Westminster Bank Sailing Club and is the Power Cruising Section representative to the General Committee of the Club. He is a holder of the French Inland Waterways 'Certificat de Capacité' and has been power cruising on the canals, Broads and Thames as well as on the Continent for a number of years in addition to sail cruising and racing at sea. He is now studying for the Board of Trade's Yachtmaster's (Coastal) Certificate. He works for National Westminster Bank as Editorial Assistant of the Bank's house magazine.

R. E. CHASE

is Honorary Secretary of the Power Cruising Section of the National Westminster Bank Sailing Club, which he joined after a number of years as Secretary of a small motor cruising club which operated on the Thames. He has devoted countless hours to encouraging young people to go afloat on the inland waterways and has spent his spare time over a number of years on the Thames or Broads in numerous types of cruiser. During the working week he serves in one of the Bank's branches in the home counties.

When not working for the Bank or organising Club cruises both Chris Cove-Smith and Bob Chase can often be found on the Thames in the season giving instruction to, and piloting hire cruiser customers through their first lock.

Pilotage

on

Inland Waterways

BOATING is booming everywhere – but nowhere so explosively as on the rivers and canals of this country. Getting afloat, particularly on the canals, seems so simple; and so much has been written about the beauty and interest of our inland waterways that the temptation to go exploring is irresistible.

Most books on the subject devote a few pages, or even a chapter, to boat handling. Here, however, we have in one volume a complete guide to pilotage on the inland waterways – which in fact is an art of its own needing as many, if different, skills as those possessed by the salt-water sailor.

This is a book which not only enumerates and explains the rules and customs of navigation on river and canal, but also how to handle a boat so that the rules may be adhered to. It also lists essential equipment and its use – much of which again differs from maritime practice.

Pilotage on Inland Waterways was compiled by C. Cove-Smith and R. E. Chase for the benefit of members of the club to which both authors belong. It is, however, too important a manual to be confined to a limited readership, and is now to be available to everyone who loves and uses the waterways of the United Kingdom.

Charles E. Jones

Contents

Chapter

Appendices

Acknowledgements

We would like to acknowledge with grateful thanks the help and advice from the following persons and organisations who have so freely given us the benefit of their expert advice in the compilation of the manual.

Lawrence Cameron, Bernard Cove-Smith, Lt. Cmdr. Paul Satow (River Superintendent – P.L.A.), H. F. Brooker, Peter Zivy and Ted Johnson (S.A.I.N.T. Line Cruisers), J. N. Curry and J. J. O'Connor (Irish Hire Boat Operators Ltd.), H. J. V. Hilditch (Willow Wren Hire Cruisers Ltd.), B. H. T Bushnell (Bert Bushnell (Maidenhead) Ltd.), J. R. Manning, R. E. Eyles, A. E. Drabble, Bryan F. Pocock, H. W. Ward, Hugh McKnight.

Newage Marine Limited, The Thames Conservancy, The Inland Waterways Association Limited, The British Waterways Board, The Port of London Authority, Antifyre Limited and the Royal Yachting Association.

Our publishers' advice and help has also been instrumental in ensuring that no stone has been left unturned in the presentation of what we hope will be a work of reference to all who enjoy their leisure on the inland waters of this and many other countries.

Preface

With the increasing interest in sailing in all its forms, motor yachting has grown, perhaps more than any other branch of the sport, as it can appeal to the whole family and, on the inland waterways, is as safe and pleasant a way of spending a summer holiday as any.

With the increase in the number of boats, unfortunately have come the problems of overcrowding of the more popular waterways, such as the River Thames and the Norfolk Broads, although in recent years considerable interest has been aroused in the 1,000 odd miles of waterways which form our canal network, which, at present, is far from crowded.

For these two reasons, we feel that it is important that the master or helmsman of a motor yacht or power cruiser should be competent to handle his craft. In respect of crowded waterways his competency should be of the highest order and in respect of the lesser used waterways he will have to be independent and self-reliant since help and advice may be more difficult to obtain.

To those who are already adherents of this revival in inland waterway cruising and to those who are perhaps hesitant to take the responsibility of navigating a cruiser along some of the most delightful waterways in the world, this manual is dedicated.

The first edition was originally written for the National Westminster Bank Sailing Club, Power Cruising Section whose members, interested in inland waterway cruising had asked the authors to recommend a book on the subject. We could only recommend half a dozen or so to amply cover the whole range of topics that pilotage and cruiser management covers. Bearing in mind that the Royal Yachting Association itemised certain inland waterway subjects in their National Motor Launch and Powerboat Certificate syllabus and that waterway authorities are continually pressing for more responsible behaviour by navi-

1

gators of their rivers and canals, we have completely revised the manual to cover the above syllabus and as many authorities' bye-laws as we could lay hands on in so far as they relate to pilotage on the inland waterways.

Basically, the manual is designed to cater for the owner or hirer of a single screw motor cruiser of up to forty feet in length or a converted narrow boat which has a standard length of seventy feet. Notes have been added for those having twin engined, twin screw installations which will be found on page 57.

We have also been very conscious of the existence of Bye-law 9 in the British Waterways Board's General Canal Bye-Laws in our researches :

'Every vessel navigated on any canal shall have in attendance an adequate and competent crew.'

National Westminster Bank Sailing Club,
Power Cruising Section.
London, E.C.2.
C. COVE-SMITH
R. E. CHASE

Symbols

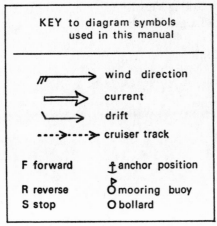

Fig. 1

NOTE

References to relevant bye-laws in this manual are in respect of those made currently at the time of going to press. Readers are strongly recommended to obtain copies of the bye-laws from the respective authorities before attempting passages in their own craft. Hire-craft operators have copies of the current bye-laws and usually incorporate the relevant instructions in their brochures, craft log-books or manuals.

References to the International Regulations for Preventing Collisions at Sea are to those adopted by the International Conference on Safety of Life at Sea, London, 1960 and presented to Parliament in July 1963. (Cmnd. 1949) H.M.S.O. 3s. These regulations have now been adopted by the U.K. Government.

SECTION I

RULE OF THE RIVER AND CANAL

'Rule of the River'
Giving Way to Sailing Vessels
Giving Way to Larger Vessels
Regattas
Commercial Craft
Anglers
Swimmers
Navigation Lights
Dredgers
Sound Signals
Speed Limits
Overtaking
Buoyage
Summary

Illustrations

4

SECTION I

RULE OF THE RIVER

Remember that the PORT side of your cruiser is to your left as you stand at the wheel or tiller facing forward. STARBOARD is on your right.

Always navigate slightly to the right of the centre of the river or canal so that you can easily pass any oncoming vessel PORT to PORT, i.e. on your left-hand side unless otherwise as signified below.

This rule may, of course, be varied according to conditions under which craft may be met, so that you should never cut across the bow of an oncoming vessel to try and pass it port to port if it would obviously be easier and safer to pass on its STARBOARD side. If you are in any doubt, signal your intention in plenty of time, either by hand or on your horn.

Small craft not under power are not controlled by this rule.

In lock cuts on rivers you must proceed in single file. Overtaking is dangerous in many instances and is expressly prohibited on the Thames.

Always give way at bends, bridges or in restricted channels to craft proceeding downstream. They are not as easily manoeuvrable as craft proceeding upstream. This rule, however is varied in tidal waters for obvious reasons. Always give way in this case to craft navigating *with* the tide.

Power vessels should always give way :
    (a) to sailing vessels, i.e. yachts, sailing barges or dinghies,
    (b) to much larger vessels which require room to manoeuvre or the course of a dredged or deep channel,
    (c) to regattas and other official river or canal functions.

(a) GIVING WAY TO SAILING VESSELS

It is a distinct advantage to the Master or Helmsman if he understands the principles which dictate the course a sailing vessel will follow.

Broadly speaking, if the wind is blowing in the same direction as the course of the river WITH the direction of travel of a yacht or dinghy the craft will be 'running'. She may be flying a spinnaker, the great balloon shaped sail which spreads forward from the mast or may have her jib (foresail) and mainsail sheeted out on opposite sides of the mast. In this case the jib is supported at its clew (the lower rear corner) by a 'whisker pole' extending from the base of the mast. The helmsman of the sailing vessel will probably maintain such a course with ease and, if in the centre of the stream the rule of passing PORT to PORT will probably apply. If overtaking, give plenty of warning and follow the helmsman's direction as to which side you may pass.

If the wind is blowing against the direction of travel of a sailing vessel, since it cannot sail directly into the wind it will have to tack from side to side on 'close hauls' whether the wind is behind you (passing) or ahead (overtaking). Whichever manoeuvre you are to execute, passing or overtaking, slow down, stop or go into reverse. DO NOT cross to the wrong side of the river. Always keep your correct station. Wait for the sailing vessel to go about, i.e. turn, on your side of the channel, keeping well clear, especially if she is upstream of you or upwind. As soon as the sailing vessel approaches the centre of the river, increase throttle and steam ahead while the yacht approaches the opposite bank and goes about again, (Fig. 2).

If the sailing vessel is 'close-hauled' but the course of the river or the wind does not dictate the use of short reaches by the sailing vessel, study the course set in relation to the wind direction which will be indicated by her burgee or pennant. Remember that she cannot sail head to wind, so that if she is approaching this condition her helmsman will soon be altering course. Keep well clear and watch for the helmsman's signal. If he has not seen you, give the appropriate sound signal, (q.v.).

Where the wind is across the river, i.e. blowing from bank to bank, sailing vessels are more able to make slight alterations of course. This point of sailing is referred to as 'reaching' and the same rule as explained at the end of the previous paragraph would apply.

Remember that the rule states that power vessels MUST give way to sailing vessels. In giving way, SLOW DOWN, STOP, or REVERSE. *NEVER* alter course violently or cross to the wrong side of the stream, unless the helmsman of the sailing vessel or a race official has indicated that you may pass him on that side, and then only follow his instruction if it is absolutely safe for you to do so.

These foregoing notes are mostly applicable to the Rivers Thames and Trent and the Norfolk and Suffolk Broads where a number of sailing clubs are located or, in the latter case, where sailing craft are available in small numbers for hire.

(b) GIVING WAY TO LARGER VESSELS

Since this manual is primarily concerned with the average river cruiser of up to 40 feet in length or canal cruiser which may be up to 70 feet in length the definition of a larger vessel may be taken as one having a draft, width or length which necessitates her being navigated with extreme care and in well-defined channels at reduced speed. Certain large craft not covered by this definition should also be treated with similar respect, since their size and weight alone would render extensive damage to a pleasure cruiser in the event of a collision.

Even when moving slowly, a coastal vessel or barge tends to draw small craft towards its bows or sides and push them aside close to the stern by virtue of the thrust of their propellers. Stay well clear, but do not go too close to the bank whilst

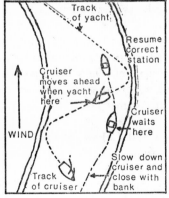

Fig. 2. Passing a tacking sailing vessel

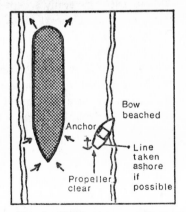

Fig. 3. Giving way to a larger vessel. (The arrows indicate propeller thrust)

7

under power, as, on the approach of a large vessel, the water level will drop, especially in a narrow channel and you may even temporarily go aground. Should your engine stall at the crucial moment, or if you consider it would be sensible to shut off power while the larger vessel passes you, beach your own craft's bow in the bank, so that the cruiser forms an angle with the bank as shown in Fig. 3, thus leaving the stern gear out in deeper water. It is also a good idea to use the mud-weight or anchor over the stern to stop it swinging and, if possible, to post a member of the crew ashore with a warp made fast to one of the stern cleats, the other end held or, preferably hitched to a post or tree as shown.

(c) REGATTAS, ETC.

Precedence should be given to regattas and official river functions, where racing is probably taking place. Remember that in any case you must give way to sailing vessels or small craft such as rowing boats, skiffs, punts or canoes which you would expect to find at such events. Look out for Regatta Officials who will give you directions if necessary. These should be followed carefully and courteously and are probably given for your own safety as well as that of others.

COMMERCIAL CRAFT

Although it is generally accepted as being an unwritten rule, we quote from the General Canal Bye-Laws of the British Waterways Board, Bye-Law 19 (1) of which states 'A pleasure boat when meeting, overtaking or being overtaken by a power-driven vessel other than a pleasure boat shall as far as possible keep out of the main navigable channel.' This supports the practice of pleasure craft giving precedence to commercial craft, which is particularly important on commercially used navigations such as the Rivers Severn, Trent and Thames, also the Yare on the Broads and the Aire and Calder, Sheffield and South Yorkshire and Weaver Navigations. Narrow boats, barges, (sailing and power) coasters, tugs and composite craft (i.e. trains of barges or craft towed by a tug) should always be accorded precedence wherever possible. This rule also applies to passenger carrying launches which run to a time-table such as those operated by Salter Bros. on the Thames.

Masters and owners of such craft are usually paid 'per cargo', except in the latter case so that the maxim 'time is money' is very true and while little delay is experienced in according precedence in the matter of passing or overtaking and although the rule does not specify that one should give way at a lock, it is at a lock (or swing or lift bridge, etc.) that your giving precedence to such a vessel will be very greatly appreciated. 'Queue-jumping,' on the other hand may be an exhilarating sport but a barge- or tug-master can be a valuable friend if you get into difficulties so that it pays to gain a reputation for being courteous and even surrendering a place in a queue. Again, you must remember also that when locking through a manned lock or a lock at which a Waterway official is present such official (or lock-keeper) is entitled to determine the order of entry into the lock, of the craft waiting outside. DO NOT argue with a lock-keeper. Most of them have been at it for years and know more about their job than we ever will.

Barge-masters, lock-keepers and watermen will respect you far more for your help in following their directions or giving precedence to their craft than if you insist on your 'rights' when they meet you. As the master of a pleasure craft you may find that you have fewer rights in these matters than you suppose.

ANGLERS

Fishermen claim as much right to the use of many waterways as the cruising man. This is reasonable as many of them have to pay for the privilege, although riparian owners (those who own the land that abuts the waterway) may enjoy fishing rights as a common law or statutory interest. On some canals the British Waterways Board has even declared prohibitions on the movement of craft at certain times for the sake of fishermen, a matter which has aroused a good deal of controversy. Why the human species cannot enjoy their leisure occupation in harmony with others is a mystery but it is probably through the non-observance of reasonable and considerate behaviour on the part of either angler or helmsman that friction has arisen.

When passing anglers on the bank, (or sitting in a punt off the bank secured to fishing stakes as in France) slow down and ensure that no wash is created whatsoever. Gentlemen who sit in punts in the middle of the river are different game. We regret that tne authors have little sympathy with them and doubt that they can claim any rights, since their presence is often a hindrance to navigation.

If you wish to stop and fish and hold the necessary licence (where required), make certain that you are not obstructing important notices or navigation marks. Tying up to, or within 20 yards of a channel marker is dangerous, thoughtless and damned bad manners. We have seen a power cruiser grounded because a channel marker was obscured by a moored cruiser, fishing.

Keep an eye open for floats and lines. Angling equipment is costly and lines fouled round your propeller can lead to trouble.

SWIMMERS

Watch out for swimmers and bathers. Guide maps to a large scale usually show the normal bathing places, especially on the rivers and broads. The fact that the water may not look very inviting to you as a boating enthusiast does not mean that everyone else has condemned the idea of taking a dip. Rivers, such as the Thames, where pollution is carefully controlled, are quite safe for bathing in parts. Slow down, or even stop, until you are quite certain that bathers have seen you and are well clear of your channel. Use your horn if you have to. A swimmer's hearing is often impaired by water and the sound of your engine may be insufficient to warn him of your approach. Bathing in canals is rarely permitted.

GENERAL

If your way ahead is not clear – SLOW DOWN, STOP, or REVERSE. When clear, proceed ahead slowly. DO NOT turn or change course without making sure it is clear or that neighbouring vessels are fully aware of your intentions.

NAVIGATION LIGHTS

Before proceeding at night, make sure that you are legally permitted to do so under the bye-laws or regulations of the authority who control the waterway. In cases of hire-craft the usual form of charter agreement applicable to pleasure cruisers excludes the ability to navigate during the hours of darkness, a condition usually imposed by the owners' insurers. Failure to observe this condition makes the contract voidable and in any case the required lights are not usually provided, so that you will be contravening the bye-laws anyway if you do move the craft at night.

The usual regulations for craft navigating at night vary between river and canal slightly but the basic requirements are illustrated in Fig. 4. For river and main commercial waterway work the requirements are as follows: On the mast or staff at the bow a bright white light visible through an arc of 225 degrees forward at a height not less than 4 feet above the hull should be displayed. On the STARBOARD side a green light should show, visible through an arc of 112½ degrees from right ahead to two points abaft the starboard beam. On the PORT side a red light should be similarly displayed from right ahead to two points abaft the port beam. On the stern a white light should be positioned visible through an arc of 135 degrees aft. Tricolour or bicolour units will not normally satisfy the requirements of most authorities. They ARE made and may be economic to purchase, but remember that your own safety may depend solely on your navigation lights one night.

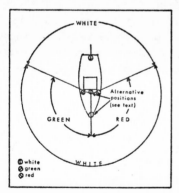

Fig. 4. Navigation lights arcs of visibility

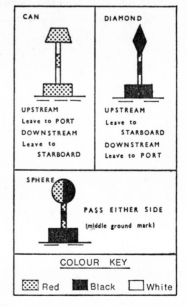

Fig. 5. Thames Buoyage system

11

In the above description the definition of 'visible' may be taken as 'visible on a dark night with a clear atmosphere at a distance of at least one mile'. The PORT and STARBOARD lights are not compulsorily required by the British Waterways Board on the non-commercial cruiseways and the requirements for a narrow canal boat are modified to a 'visible white light, displayed in the forepart of the vessel, where it can best be seen and at a height above the deck or gunwhale of not less than one foot'. The coloured sidelights are, however required for the commercial navigations such as the Trent, Weaver, Aire and Calder, New Junction Canal and the Sheffield and South Yorkshire Navigation (below Doncaster).

The bye-laws of the respective authorities should also be consulted for details of special circumstances where differing systems of lights are displayed, i.e. by 'composite craft', dredgers and tugs, so that these can be recognised at night.

For movement at night you will also require some sort of searchlight. Specialist firms offer many models but an ordinary 'Lucas' motor-car spotlight can be used, mounted on a swivel on the wheelhouse roof unless navigation in commercial waterways is envisaged, when it would probably be prudent to invest in rather more substantial equipment.

The spotlight is also a necessity for canal tunnel work. When negotiating a tunnel it is good practice to switch on your navigation lights if carried, so that oncoming craft are aware of your presence. In this country you are obliged by the bye-laws to display a white light forward in any tunnel exceeding a quarter of a mile in length. In France, full navigation lights should be shown.

To use the spotlight to best advantage, focus the beam on to the wall on either side of the tunnel about 100 yards ahead of the vessel's bow. If the towpath extends through the tunnel, choose the wall on the towpath side and allow the lower part of the beam to illuminate the towpath so that you can see the 'kerb'. The helmsman should look well ahead, concentrating on keeping the beam moving evenly along the tunnel wall.

DREDGERS
On approaching dredgers or craft engaged in piling or diving operations you *must* slow down. Clear passage will be indicated

12

on the craft by means of a white diamond 18 in. x 18 in. minimum size displayed on that side of the craft or obstruction on which you may pass. The side on which work is being carried out or which is impassable will be denoted by a red diamond. At night, lights are displayed in triangular form, the base of the triangle containing one white and one red light, the side of the triangle having the red light indicating the closed channel. Certain authorities may only use similarly coloured flags, French dredgers vary slightly in that the day-marks are discs in similar colours, which are replaced at night by coloured lights, white and red. (See also Section on 'Cruising in France').

SOUND SIGNALS
The sound signals used in this country are based on the International Collision Prevention Regulations although the definitions differ slightly :

SIGNAL	INLAND WATERWAY DEFINITION (and see various bye-laws)	INTERNATIONAL REGULATIONS DEFINITION
1 Short Blast	I am directing my course to STARBOARD	I am altering course to STARBOARD
2 Short Blasts	I am directing my course to PORT	I am altering course to PORT
3 Short Blasts	My engines are going ASTERN	My engines are going ASTERN
4 Short Blasts	I am unable to manoeuvre	—
4+1 Short Blasts	I am turning round to STARBOARD	—
4+2 Short Blasts	I am turning round to PORT	—
5 or more Short Blasts	You are not taking sufficient action to avoid me	You are not taking sufficient action to avoid me

The fifth and sixth signals should be sounded with a slight pause after the fourth blast. They are written into the Thames Conservancy bye-laws but are only accepted practice among commercial craft on the lower reaches of that authority's area. They are no longer contained in the Port of London Authority

Bye-laws, although they may still appear in some almanacs. Note that in the third definition that it is only IMPLIED that the craft is stopping. A power cruiser or ship with engines going astern is not easily manoeuvrable, so that you should be doubly on guard if in the vicinity of a vessel which has made his signal.

Give warnings in plenty of time. Do not use any other 'codes' unless you are aware that the bye-laws require them, except, perhaps, one long blast of four to six seconds' duration to give warning of approach or when leaving a mooring if this is strictly necessary. Always listen for other boats' signals, especially if your view of the waterway is restricted, as at bends, bridges etc. Unnecessary use of the horn will, however, give you a rotten name on the river.

SPEED LIMITS

Speed limits are either suggested or fixed by certain river and canal authorities, either over the whole length of the waterway or over certain portions. These are notified by signboards at locks or appropriate places where restrictions commence. In general a suggested speed limit on rivers is 7 knots (8 m.p.h.) although on narrow canals and other waterways controlled by the British Waterways Board you must not exceed 4 m.p.h. and in many cases this will be less. THE GUIDING FACTOR IS THAT YOU MUST PROCEED AT A SPEED WHICH WILL *NOT CREATE EXCESSIVE WASH* AT THE BANK or swell which will inconvenience other waterway users, particularly those at moorings or in smaller craft. At bends, approaching locks, bridges, dredgers, etc., proceed slowly under power but at a speed to give sufficient steerage way to manoeuvre. ALWAYS give way to craft proceeding DOWN-STREAM or WITH THE TIDE at such places.

OVERTAKING

Make certain that the river is clear. Overtake on the PORT side of the craft ahead if it is to your STARBOARD which is to be preferred, but you may overtake on the STARBOARD side if there is room. In accordance with the International Regulations as adopted by some authorities' bye-laws, the over-taking vessel is required to give sound signals as set out on

14

page 13, i.e. to overtake to PORT you should sound two short blasts. The same signal should be given by the overtaken vessel as an acknowledgement and vice versa. If it is dangerous to overtake then the vessel you intend to overtake will sound one of the other appropriate signals such as five short and rapid blasts.

If you are being overtaken, maintain your course and speed. DO NOT accelerate. This is bad manners and may we venture to suggest, rather childish.

BUOYAGE

Inland Waterways can be deceptive in their appearance in that the water from bank to bank may not cover a logical bed, deeper in the centre and sloping up uniformly to the sides. It will be shown elsewhere that there are well known variations which are quite predictable by the experienced Pilot, but in certain cases otherwise the layout of the river bed may not be in accordance with the usual geological rules.

It is here that the responsible authority may elect to mark the channel by means of buoys which float but are securely moored to the river bed. They can, therefore rise and fall with the tide or river level, but have the inherent disadvantage that they cannot be used to pinpoint an object below the surface as accurately as marker posts, which are also sometimes used and can, of course, be driven vertically into the river bed. Fig. 5 shows the shapes used and colours of the buoys used by the Thames Conservancy and which conform to International agreements. All buoys are shown as they appear to craft proceeding UP-STREAM. Remember, therefore that buoys should be passed on the opposite hand to that shown when proceeding downstream or AGAINST the flood tide, (that is – WITH the ebb). Marker posts are usually similarly coloured to the buoys.

In addition mention should be made of buoys marking wrecks. These are now internationally agreed as being coloured green. The correct hand for passing them is dictated by the shapes as above. A can should be left to PORT, a diamond or cone to STARBOARD and a sphere may be passed on either side.

Buoys may or may not be lit. Port hand buoys show either a red light which may give up to four flashes in any one cycle or may show a white light flashing in groups of 2, 4 or 6. Star-

15

board hand buoys show a white light flashing in groups of 1, 3 or 5.

In tidal reaches of a river a number of variations of buoyage may be found but the above are the guiding principles. If you contemplate working in tidal waters, such as the Thames below Teddington, it is imperative that you obtain Reed's Almanac for constant reference aboard and also that you have studied a certain amount of Coastal Navigation. It would be infinitely more preferable to have an experienced seaman aboard than risk your vessel through lack of knowledge. Such port authorities as the Port of London Authority, whose jurisdiction covers the whole of the tidal estuary of the Thames are not averse to the responsible enquiries of amateur yachtsmen. They will appreciate your concern and be grateful for a request for help prior to any passage of the area which you contemplate, rather than having to come to your assistance in an emergency caused by thoughtless actions which may well endanger commercial shipping or lives.

Such authorities normally issue their own bye-laws and these should be purchased well in advance if you are to visit their area.

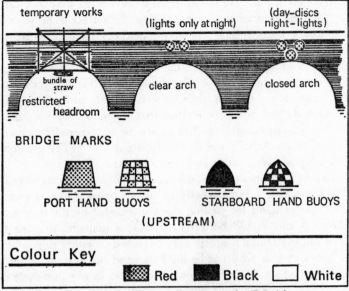

Fig. 6. Some Thames Estuary marks (P.L.A.)

16

SUMMARY

The notes given below, summarise mainly what has been discussed in this section. Since they are compiled from the 'Code of Conduct' issued by the British Waterways Board you are, however, advised to read them carefully as they cover certain points peculiar to canal navigation which are not applicable to other types of waterway.

1. Commercial craft must always be given priority – they are working boats for which the canal system in particular was created.

2. The 'Rules of the Road' are:

(a) Craft meeting from opposite directions: each steer to STARBOARD, so that they pass 'PORT to PORT' (left side to left side).

(b) Exception – if conditions make it impossible to follow the rule above craft must give two short blasts on their horn to indicate their intention to steer to PORT and pass 'STARBOARD to STARBOARD'.

(c) Craft overtaking another going in the same direction: the overtaking craft to pass with its STARBOARD side nearest to the overtaken craft (the latter steering to STARBOARD as necessary to facilitate passing). On broad rivers and waterways this rule may be varied according to circumstances.

(d) Exception – craft meeting or overtaking another vessel being towed from the bank should always pass 'outside' the towed vessel, never between it and the bank from which it is being towed, for obvious reasons. There are even exceptions again to this rule, but do not concern us, since they apply to the meeting of two vessels, both under tow from the bank.

3. Observe speed limits at all times and specially slow down when approaching or passing:

(a) moored craft, (b) tunnels, narrow bridges etc., (c) engineering works.

When the view ahead is obstructed or visibility is reduced, you should also sound a prolonged blast on your horn at 20-second intervals until clear, although in the latter case you should moor up to the bank immediately. Commercial craft may continue to navigate in fog or thick mist. Do not try to copy them.

17

4. On bends, slow down and navigate towards the outside (which is usually deeper), but keep a close look-out for other craft doing the same. If you are on the 'wrong' side of the stream you will have to give way.

5. Keep a good look-out for danger and obstruction notices, or red flags which usually denote temporary obstructions.

6. In tunnels more than 440 yards long all craft must display at least a white light.

SECTION II

CONTROLS

The Helm
The Gear Lever
The Throttle
Combined Gear and Throttle
Brakes
Clutch
Starting and Stopping the Petrol Engine
Starting and Stopping the Diesel Engine
Engine Running
Summary (Check lists)

Illustrations

SECTION II

THE CONTROLS OF A CRUISER

The primary controls of an inboard engined single screw cruiser are 1. The helm or wheel, 2. The gear lever and, 3. The throttle. Secondary controls cover the ignition switch, choke, starter, horn and various accessory switches etc., where fitted.

THE HELM

The commonest form of helm control aboard a cruiser is the wheel. On a smaller cruiser or auxiliary sailer a tiller may only be provided where the control position is at the stern. This arrangement also applies to the conventional narrow boat and many conversions of this type of craft for pleasure use. Some purpose built narrow canal pleasure craft place the wheel in a centre wheel-house, a practice that the authors doubt as being the best as, in view of the length of a conventional narrow boat, the stern steering and control positions seem to recommend themselves as they give an easy overall view of the craft to the helmsman.

The conventional wheel has the inner spokes carried through the rim to provide hand-holds outside the circumference. In the days of the big sailing ships, these spokes were essential so that the helmsmen could apply their full weight to turning the ship under the terrific stress of a full spread of canvas on four, five and even six masts. Some builders now provide car-type steering wheels without the exterior spokes and these are perfectly adequate. Some wheels are provided with a grip handle set at right angles to the wheel rim, positioned at 'top dead centre' when the wheel is in the 'rudder ahead' position. This is to facilitate fast turning of the helm when manoeuvring and turning at slow speeds.

Remember that the top spokes of the wheel move towards the direction in which the bow will swing when running ahead and away from that direction when running astern. Conversely, a tiller bar, fitted direct to the rudder stock moves away from the direction the bow will swing when moving ahead. However, since it is situated in the stern it may be easier to remember that the tiller moves in the same direction as the swing of the STERN when running ahead. Tiller bars are more common and infinitely more preferable on a narrow boat or narrow boat conversion, especially if of the conventional full length of 70 feet, due to the special handling characteristics of the narrow boat which are discussed in the next section.

The wheel is connected by wires or rods and universal joints to the stock of the rudder which is rotated by a quadrant, having stops on either side to prevent the rudder being turned too far. Lock to lock revolutions vary with the gearing and diameter of the working part of the wheel hub but usually runs out at between four and six revolutions. Do not heave at the wheel once it is at its stop thinking you will get it further over. You will probably break the stop and in some cases reverse the rudder, seriously damaging it in the propeller.

THE GEAR LEVER

The gear lever on older craft is a separate control, although more recently for reasons which will become more apparent this is often incorporated with the throttle. There are three positions for the gear, forward, neutral and reverse. Do not operate the gear lever when the engine is running any faster than tick-over speed. Even in an emergency the engine speed must be reduced to tick-over before a new gear is selected. Always operate the gear lever firmly. The normal procedure when changing from forward to reverse is therefore :
1. Close throttle.
2. Pull lever out of forward gear and push firmly into reverse.
3. Open throttle.

Proceeding from reverse to forward is treated in a similar manner. Gear levers normally push forward or up to engage forward gear and pull to the rear or down to engage reverse gear. Individual boats may vary according to engine layout circumstances and a new helmsman should always enquire the gear 'shift' arrangements before piloting a cruiser as a matter of extreme importance. One of us nearly demolished the top gate of Boulters Lock with a cruiser through not making this enquiry.

Levers may be floor mounted or in the panel beside the helmsman's seat. More modern ones are often fixed beside the dash-board.

THE THROTTLE
Unlike the motor-car which requires constant changes of speed when being driven along the road a cruiser is best operated at an optimum fixed speed when not manoeuvring and a simple hand control, usually fitted close to the dashboard or even mounted on it is provided. The lever provides tick-over at its bottom position, the optimum cruising speed being somewhere between one half and two thirds of the maximum travel. Above this optimum engine revolutions will be increased, but due to propeller and hull design the cruiser will not travel much faster in proportion. You will unnecessarily increase fuel consumption, invite clutch slip and over a period of time increase engine wear. Remember too that inland waterway authorities lay down speed limits and frown seriously on undue swell or wash in the wake of a cruiser. Some hire cruiser engines are governed so that pushing the throttle to its highest position is a waste of the fractional effort involved anyway. Lever fittings are either semi-stiff, remaining in whichever position they are set or free, the latter usually being threaded and provided with a knurled ring which can be screwed down on to the slot escutcheon to clamp the lever in any desired position.

COMBINED GEAR AND THROTTLE
To prevent accidental changes of gear at high revs, the combined gear and throttle system is gaining wider popularity with marine engineers. A 'Clutch' may or may not be provided. Several types are marketed relying on either rods or Bowden cables for linkage to the engine. More sophisticated types use hydraulic lines similar to those for car brake and clutch systems.
The principle is that the lever is positioned in a vertical slot and when centred in the halfway position runs the engine at tick-over, the gear being in neutral. Small movement up the slot engages forward gear and further travel increases engine speed. A small movement down from centre engages reverse gear and further travel down increases engine speed again. Thus it is impossible to change gear without reducing the engine to tick-over speed. Always pause slightly when changing

22

from one gear to the other. Some controls dispense with the slot, having the lever mounted on a hub protruding from the control gear casing but the principle is exactly the same.

All controls of this pattern are of the semi-stiff type.

BRAKES

There are *NO* brakes. Remember this. It is very important.

CLUTCH

The separate gear lever operates the clutch as part of the gear changing cycle, drawing the clutch apart when being moved back from forward and then operating the actual gear cogs and shafts in the gear-box to the neutral position with the clutch down. It should always be stressed to a helmsman that the lever should be pushed fully home in either direction to make sure, not that the gear cogs are fully engaged but that the clutch dogs are in positive contact. Marine clutches are not used to the constant demands as found in the motor car and are not therefore usually so robust. Certain types consist merely of two cones, one biting on the inside of the other. Failure to push them fully home turns the inner cone into an effective drill which promptly wears the other down, and an early replacement is necessary, to say nothing of the impaired performance of the propeller due to clutch slip. The remarks of course, only apply to the separate gear type of installation.

There is another type of 'clutch' which is found only on the combined gear and throttle control of the 'Morse' or 'Teleflex' type and is used to alter the operation of the control from gear/throttle to throttle only. This facilitates the running of the engine for warming up or battery charging out of gear. The control is on the gear control casing at the base of the lever and consists of a knob which is operated by pulling out to disengage the gear section. Pressed home the control works as described under 'Combined Gear and Throttle'.

The 'Teleflex' control varies slightly in that the disengagement of the clutch from the throttle is effected by pressing a button down on top of the control hub. The button only remains down whilst the lever is operating in the 'forward' or 'reverse' positions and resets itself into the 'engaged' position when the lever is moved to 'tickover/neutral'. Older patterns have a recess containing the button; later models are as shown in Fig. 7.

ENGINE PROCEDURES

Briefly stated – Petrol engines are lighter, cheaper to buy and possibly easier to obtain fuel for on the river. Conversely, fuel is much dearer for petrol than for diesel, power for power a petrol engine gives lower M.P.G. or H.P.G. (Hours per gallon) and petrol vapour has a lower flash point than diesel oil vapour. On a boat using Calor Gas, the risk of explosion is therefore more prevalent if gas has escaped and is ignited by the petrol engine's high tension system. Diesel engines are heavier than their petrol counterparts but therefore more solid and perhaps longer lasting. They are dearer to buy and instal but cheaper to run. Having no high tension system risk of gas explosion is not as great.

STARTING THE PETROL ENGINE
The gear lever must be in neutral. Turn on the fuel, presumably having dipped the tank. Note that a fuel tank should never fall below the $1\frac{1}{2}/2$ gallon mark or air may enter the fuel line and prevent the engine running at anything faster than tick-over, out of gear, if at all. From cold use choke by pulling it half out or more and set the throttle only at about quarter open. Switch on ignition and operate starter. If engine fires leave starter and adjust choke and throttle to give a fairly fast tick-over. If an engine does not fire, the usual checks for a car engine should be carried out : fuel, battery state, dry and clean plugs, tight leads, distributor head, condenser, timing etc. If the cooling is of the primary and secondary circuit type with a heat exchanger check that the header tank for fresh water is full. To stop engine : Turn off the ignition.

Then turn off the fuel, if it will not be required again for a few hours or more.

STARTING THE DIESEL ENGINE
The gear lever must be in neutral. Make sure the stop button, lever or knob is not raised. This prevents fuel being delivered to the injectors. Switch on ignition and if starting from cold

24

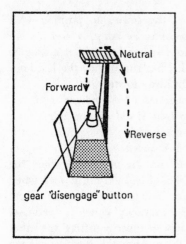

Fig. 7. 'Teleflex' control

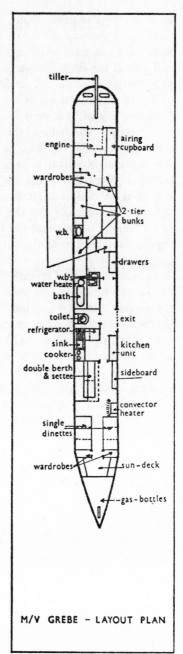

M/V GREBE - LAYOUT PLAN

Fig. 8. Narrow boat conversion

25

turn the two position switch of the starter to position 1 or 'Preheat' for about 10 to 15 seconds. A lamp or coil on the dashboard will start to glow. Move switch to position 2. Engine will fire. If the engine is warm i.e. has run during the last hour or so, switch to position 2 straight away to start it.

If a diesel fails to fire it is suggested expert advice is sought. Some engines will not start from cold, if old and have lost their compression. To reduce the compression flashpoint in the cylinders ether vapour can be introduced by means of a proprietary aerosol which is squirted up the air intake when the starter is operated. The throttle should be held fairly open when this is done. On an installation having combined 'gear and throttle' control make sure the 'throttle only' clutch is operative. If no 'clutch' is provided the crew member squirting the ether vapour into the air intake should operate the throttle linkage on the engine itself which will not disturb the gear control.

To stop engine : Operate the cut-out knob. Not until the engine has completely stopped should the knob be returned to the 'engine running' position. TURN OFF THE IGNITION. Do not forget on a diesel boat, the engine is not turned off by turning off the ignition. Neither does the fact that the engine is not running indicate that the ignition is off. Do NOT turn off the fuel. An airlock in the fuel line of a diesel installation is a serious matter. Do not invite trouble.

As soon as an engine has fired and is running, check the oil pressure. This pressure varies according to the age and condition of the engine but a starting pressure of less than 30–35 lbs. per sq. inch (2.110–2.461 kilogrammes per sq. cm.) in an engine in reasonable condition is not normally acceptable. In any event you will probably be advised by your boatyard or the engine manufacturer of the pressure before you set off. If not, it is better to enquire than be sorry later. If the pressure is not up to standard or is nil then stop your engine at once and seek expert assistance.

Check the exhaust outlet and make sure that water is being expelled with the exhaust gases. This is most important. If no water is present, the water intake may be blocked or the strainers may require cleaning. (See Appendix on Engine Maintenance). Failure to obtain proper water circulation will result in the overheating of the engine and eventual seizure. Lack of oil pressure as discussed in the previous paragraph will have the same result.

Note that air-cooled engines, an example of which is installed in the narrow boat shown in Fig. 8 do not always expel water from their exhausts as, besides having an air-cooled engine they also have an air-cooled exhaust. We have met several worried skippers on the first morning of a cruise, fearful that a solid reliable Lister air-cooled diesel is about to blow up under their feet, as they have become so well drilled in the starting up routine checks!

CONVERSION TABLE – lb/sq. in. to kg./sq. cm.			
lb./sq."	KG/lb. sq.cm.	lb./sq."	KG/lb. sq.cm.
18	1.266	39	2.742
20	1.406	40	2.812
22	1.547	42	2.953
25	1.758	43	3.023
29	2.039	45	3.164
30	2.110	46	3.234
32	2.250	48	3.375
35	2.461	50	3.515
36	2.531	60	4.218

It is also a good idea to check the ammeter. Some boats possess a charging switch: others are provided with an automatic cut-out and voltage regulator as on a car. If on depressing the charging switch the ammeter registers 15/20 amps leave it thrown until the meter registers about 0–3 amps. When this occurs, switch the charging circuit off. Excessive or overcharging is detrimental to a battery, causing a breakdown of the plates and gassing. A battery state meter may be supplied. This is a very useful indicator but does not measure the rate of charge.

Other accessories are controlled from the dashboard and/or close to the helmsman's position. Accessories are normally electrically operated, such as the horn, navigation lights, windscreen wiper, if fitted, interior lighting, etc. Even an electric bilge pump is a refinement found on hire cruisers these days! Some bilge pumps, however, are driven straight from the engine mechanically so that no attention to this morning chore is required.

Air cooled diesel engines are quite common on narrow boats, of the type shown in Fig. 8. This particular craft, owned and operated by Willow Wren Hire Cruisers Ltd. of Rugby possesses a Lister SR3 MGR2 three-cylinder air-cooled engine with oil operated gear-box and 2:1 reduction gear, being operated by a combined gear/throttle control of the type shown in Fig. 7. There being no water circulation system utilizing river or canal water this cannot become clogged, which is a frequent occurrence, especially in little used canal sections where weed and debris are not frequently cleared. Such engines also do not have problems of ice forming in a partially drained cooling system during the winter when the boat is laid up. They also permit continued use with more reliable performance throughout the winter months, if required. Owners of air-cooled car engines will probably vouch for this.

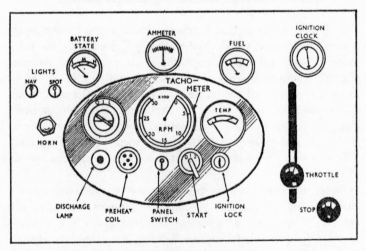

Fig. 9. Diesel cruiser dashboard lay-out (based on Saint Line Cruiser 'Ste. Claude')

SUMMARY

Given below are the summarised points of the preceding Section in the form of check lists for starting and stopping the engine of your craft. Oil and water capacities are assumed to have been checked as full. (See Appendix on Engine Maintenance.)

STARTING	
PETROL	DIESEL
1. Check fuel tank	1. Check fuel tank
2. Turn on the fuel	2. Ensure that the fuel pump cut-out is not operative. (Knob should be fully in)
3. Check that gear lever is in neutral or that the gear button is in 'disengaged' position	3. Check that gear lever is in neutral or that the gear button is in 'disengaged' position
4. Turn on ignition	4. Turn on ignition, if fitted
5. If cold, open choke half-way and leave throttle about a quarter open	5. If cold and a 2-position starter is fitted, turn lever to 'Position 1'
6. Press or pull starter	6. After 10 seconds or when indicator glows turn starter switch to 'Position 2' OR Operate starter
7. Engine fires	7. Engine fires
8. Check oil pressure	8. Check oil pressure
9. Check ammeter	9. Check ammeter
10. Switch on charging circuit, if required	10. Switch on charging circuit, if required
11. Check that water is being expelled from exhaust outlet. (*Water cooled exhausts only*)	11. Check that water is being expelled from exhaust outlet. (*Water cooled exhausts only*)
12. Engage gears as required	12. Engage gears as required

STOPPING

PETROL	DIESEL
1. Disengage gears	1. Disengage gears
2. Turn off ignition	2. Pull out pump cut-out (Stop lever or knob)
3. Remove ignition key	3. Push in cut-out when engine fully stopped
4. Turn off fuel	4. TURN OFF IGNITION if fitted
	5. Remove key

SECTION III

MANOEUVRING UNDER POWER

The Propeller
The Rudder
Current Effects
Wind Effects
Handling
Turning
Leaving a Berth
Approaching a Berth
Using the Anchor
Canal Notes
Twin Screw Vessels
Emergencies

Illustrations

SECTION III

MANOEUVRING UNDER POWER

This section deals with handling on river, broad and canal, although the latter, especially the narrow canal poses certain handling problems particularly with the conventionally lengthed narrow-boat. Canal users are therefore advised to read the special section dealing with canal work on page 55 in conjunction with the general points which follow.

*   *   *

There are two exterior major factors which affect the propulsion of a power cruiser through the water on a desired course. To understand why a cruiser will not respond precisely to the controls like a motor-car will on a road it must be realised that neither of these factors is constant. In a motor-car the wheels revolve and turn on pivots (kingpins) and axles to propel and steer the vehicle on a hard and constant surface. These considerations do not apply with a boat.

The exterior factors involved are: 1. Current, and 2. Wind effect. These two factors can again be sub-divided into: 1.(a) Current effect upon hull when stationary, 1.(b) Current effect upon hull when in motion and, 2.(a) Wind effect on stationary hull, 2.(b) Wind effect on hull moving ahead, and 2.(c) Wind effect on hull moving astern. We will deal with these after we have considered the means of propulsion and steering aboard a cruiser. We are mainly concerned in this work with a single-engined single screw vessel. Notes on twin screw vessels will be found at the end of this section.

To propel a cruiser through the variable elements mentioned above on a desired course it is provided with a propeller, primarily for moving the craft ahead and astern and a rudder, primarily for turning. However, both these pieces of equipment have certain other 'side' effects which mar or ease the handling of a cruiser as circumstances dictate.

THE PROPELLER

The single propeller installation which we are considering has been shown as being one whose blades (and shaft) turn in a clockwise – 'right-hand' direction when running ahead as viewed from the stern. This pre-supposes a typical marine engine installation with the usual reduction gear, or the use of a right-handed engine. However, you should note that the vehicle engines on which many marine engines are based turn left handed and that if no reduction gear is fitted or such an engine has not been 're-handed', the propeller will be designed to work in an anti-clockwise direction. This is most important if you are to follow and interpret the diagrams correctly. The rudder will normally be placed aft of the propeller with its stock housed on the same line amidships as the propeller shaft. It will therefore act centrally in the slipstream of the propeller.

There are five main propeller effects which concern us which have a direct bearing on the behaviour of a vessel under power. These we will deal with in turn.

1. *Forward thrust.* Drives water astern. Pushes hull ahead.

2. *Sternward thrust.* Drives water ahead. *Pulls* hull astern. These two effects are the obvious ones for which the propeller is designed.

However, further effects come into play which can be used in turning and manoeuvring the ship in conjunction with or independent of the rudder.

3. *Sideways thrust.* More noticeable with large slow-speed propellers which will be found on cruisers having 2 : 1 reduction gear or special slow revving engines; it will be noticed from Fig. 10, that since the lower section of the propeller is in deeper water it can be used rather like a paddle wheel. If the ship is stopped in the water and the propeller starts to turn, irrespective of its design it will tend to 'paddle' the stern sideways, until way is gathered, either ahead or astern. The effect disappears more rapidly when proceeding ahead than when going astern due to the design of the hull. This effect is useful when coming alongside or leaving a berth.

This effect is hardly apparent on the average hire cruiser which usually has a high revving propeller of small diameter. To achieve the effect required when manoeuvring, a short burst of power in the 'ahead' position with the helm over towards the direction of swing required by the bow will be necessary.

4. *Slipstream effect on rudder.* In the normal type of single propeller installation which we are considering, the rudder is

set in line with the propeller shaft so that the slipstream from the propeller will strike the rudder with its full force if the rudder is deflected in either direction. Since the effect of the rudder is dependent on the force of the water passing it, it will be most noticeable at high speed. Ignoring the sideways effect described in note 3 for the moment, it follows that where the propeller is turning slowly and the helm is put over, the resultant turn will be of a fairly large radius. To tighten the turning arc, therefore, it is only necessary to increase the revolutions per minute of the propeller by opening the throttle. An increase of speed in the ship will eventually follow, but if it does before the turn is completed the speed can be checked by reversing helm and putting the propeller into reverse for a short burst. This will also check the turn if your original turn was being made to port with a 'clockwise' propeller, due to the sideways thrust already described. If your original turn was to the starboard, however, this reversing action will tend to assist you.

5. *Propeller Race Effect.* If the propeller is right-handed, (clockwise) at high speeds this minor effect is sometimes noticed. Water from the port side of the vessel is gathered by the top blades of the propeller which are moving from port to starboard and carried down to strike the rudder low on its starboard face. Since it is deeper and denser than the water striking the upper port face of the rudder there is a tendency for the stern to swing to port. A slight amount of port helm is therefore necessary to counteract this. Conversely with a left handed ('anti-clock') propeller a slight amount of starboard helm would be required.

For twin screw installations : See end of this section.

THE RUDDER

When stationary with no current running the rudder will have no effect on the ship at whichever position the helm has been put. With the rudder amidships and the ship moving ahead or astern water passing the rudder will exert equal pressure on both sides and a balanced condition will prevail. No turning effect will be applied to the hull. Now suppose the rudder is moved hard in one direction or the other, out of line with the axis of the ship. Water pressure will increase on the rudder

34

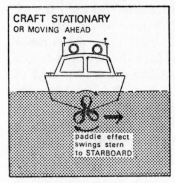

Fig. 10. Sideways thrust of propeller

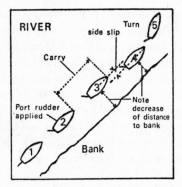

Fig. 11. Effects of applying port helm

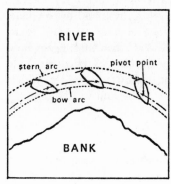

Fig. 12. Starboard turning arcs

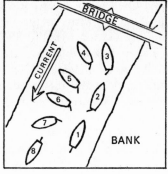

Fig. 13. Effect of current on a turn

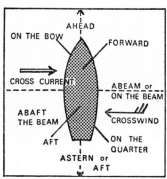

Fig. 14. Terms used in handling a cruiser etc.

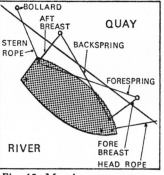

Fig. 15. Mooring rope terms

plate on the side turned in towards the stern. The first effect will be that of slowing the ship down. This is known as 'drag'.

Secondly the ship will be pushed sideways after it has carried on for any distance up to twice its length due to its momentum. This initial delay is known as the CARRY and can be calculated for any given hull in relation to its speed. It is most important to appreciate, both the initial delay and the sideways movement which will be away from the direction in which the rudder has been put. The sideways movement is most important to understand, especially if you are in confined waters. (See Fig. 11.)

Thirdly the ship will commence its turn in the desired direction, but remember that, when turning, a vessel does so on its pivot point, which varies in position from hull form to hull form. On a motor cruiser it will be generally found to be where the mast or centre of the windscreen of a centre-wheelhouse cruiser is located. (See Fig. 12.) Note that when turning the bow and stern follow different arcs since the turning effect depends on the force of water being thrust against the rudder, which is at the stern and the broadest part of the hull will be offering the most resistance to the turn.

CURRENT EFFECTS

The current of a river affects a stationary hull in a number of ways depending on whether it is moored, anchored or free. If moored to the bank it will tend to draw the bow away from the bank, if facing upstream, which is the recommended position. The craft is therefore primarily secured at the bow, secondary warps being run from the stern to the shore for additional protection. If moored, stern-on to a quay the stern warps will be under severe strain. It is therefore recommended that a long warp be taken from the bow to a position on the quay well upstream of the craft so that the warp forms at least a 40 degree angle with the craft, preferably more. (See section on Mooring.)

At anchor, a hull will swing so that its centre line is immediately downstream of the anchor, assuming the anchor hawse is near the bow.

A free floating hull, i.e. 'not under command' or more simply a vessel with stopped engines will swing to run with the current, bow first. If the vessel has been proceeding upstream and the engine cuts out it will start to run sternwards and then gradually turn broadside on. A cross wind may even turn it further to come round bow first. To prevent this rather dangerous state of affairs, the anchor should be paid out rapidly and the vessel dredged out of the way of other shipping as soon as possible. (See section on Anchor Work.)

MOVING HULL

The current will impede or assist progress according to the direction of travel of the vessel when proceeding up- or down-stream. In proceeding upstream or against the tide in a tidal waterway a vessel is infinitely more manoeuvrable, since the rudder is more sensitive at the higher speed the vessel *moves through the water*. Naturally this does not follow that this is a high speed over the ground. The rule may be equated as follows : $x = s - c$ upstream $x = s + c$ downstream, where x equals the apparent, or ground speed, s the actual water speed of the cruiser and c the speed of the current.

For example, a cruiser at 1,800 r.p.m. engine speed travels at 8 m.p.h. through the water. In a current of 2 m.p.h. it will travel at 6 m.p.h. apparent (overground) speed upstream, but at 10 m.p.h. apparent speed downstream. To achieve a uniform speed in both directions the r.p.m. of the propeller (and engine) in the downstream case will have to be reduced to give a water speed of 4 m.p.h. – an infinitely less manoeuvrable condition than that of 8 m.p.h. which is being used to propel the craft upstream. For this reason upstream always gives way to down-stream traffic.

The most dangerous effect of current and one that does not seem to be apparent to many cruiser helmsmen is felt when turning a craft in midstream. As a cruiser comes broadside on to the current the latter will increase in its effect. For this reason, if turning 'short round' or executing a three point turn always execute the manoeuvre on the DOWNSTREAM side of any obstruction such as a bridge, jetty, piling or bend. When your turn is completed you will find that the current has set you some way down stream from where you commenced to turn. (See Fig. 13.)

Up till now we have always referred to the normal river

37

current which flows from source to mouth. However, many rivers are tidal, some for a considerable distance inland. Current is therefore replaced by tide, although in some cases in the vicinity of the tidal limit of a river the two are encountered acting together or in opposition. Tides ebb (go out or recede) and flood (come in) approximately twice per day. The times of these occurrences can be predicted and the predictions are published in Almanacs and by the Admiralty each year. A table of constants, or time-lags are worked out for the major ports and points along tidal waterways so that it is not difficult for a master of a cruiser to work out the direction and possible speed of the tide at any given point in the tideway. If you wish to work in tidal waterways you must therefore obtain the necessary Almanac and tide tables applicable. It is also imperative that you know the rise and fall of the tide and the draft of your vessel. The rise and fall varies according to whether the tides are 'springs' or 'neaps' dictated by the phases of the moon. Springs create very high and very low tides, neaps giving much smaller variations in depth. Since this manual is not intended to cover tidal work, you are strongly advised to obtain a good reference book on coastal navigation. One last word of warning. Where the tide meets the current disturbed water conditions often prevail, and this section of the waterway may only be navigable at certain states of the tide. Local advice by the waterway authority in these cases is IMPERATIVE.

Mention must also be made when discussing the effects of current of the causes for its variation in speed and direction over the river bed. The main current will always follow the outside of a bend. However, it should not be assumed that it is therefore safer to navigate on the inside of the bend as, due to the lack of scouring action of a fast current, silt tends to build up on the inside and, unless your draft is very shallow, you may go aground.

In restricted channels and round islands the current will increase considerably in speed. Mention will be made in more detail of the behaviour of the current above and below a weir in the section on locks but it is as well to note here that above a weir the flow will be deceptive since the surface of the water appears undisturbed. On no account approach a weir too closely from either side. The current will set you towards the weir from above so that when passing a weir approach always calculate your course well away from it so that you can pass in safety.

On the upstream side of bridges, especially in times of flood, water tends to heap up and dangerous eddies form against the piers. Always choose your arch early and shoot straight through it.

Watch for drain, tributary and weir stream outfalls. If these are strong running, they will cause a cross-current which will set you off-course across the river if adequate precautions are not taken by the helmsman in good time. Lastly, remember the current flows more strongly IN THE CENTRE OF THE STREAM than along the banks.

WIND EFFECTS

Stationary Hull. It was stated earlier in this section that wind effects on a cruiser hull can be sub-divided into three sections, namely; wind effects on a stationary hull, and one moving ahead or astern. The degree to which the wind affects the hull varies with the design of the hull and superstructure of the vessel and, of course, the wind speed. Deep keel boats suitable for sea-cruising are more stable and not as sensitive to wind as the normal river cruiser with shallow draft and high topsides, so that if you are at the helm of the latter type of boat you must pay attention to the wind at all times.

A stationary hull will tend to turn broadside to the wind unless she is anchored in a fairly strong blow in which case she may tend to come 'bow-up' into the wind.

Moving ahead. Unfortunately, this tendency to turn broadside on to the wind also persists when moving ahead. If you are steering straight into the wind you will manage to keep on course fairly well, but as soon as the wind comes on to your bow you will have to concentrate on your steering as the craft will tend to blow off course towards either bank. If it does start to wander, move the helm slowly and watch for the swing of the bow as she goes back on course. As soon as the swing starts be prepared to meet it by bringing the helm up as though you were going to execute a turn in the opposite direction. You will feel the 'bite', a kind of extra pressure which you can retain to edge her back on course. The secret is to

39

'steer small', that is, never get impatient for a correction at the wheel to respond and push it further over. A good helmsman never spins his wheel at full speed unless he wants to turn right round in a hurry, to pick up a man overboard or his wife's washing up bowl.

With the wind blowing on to your beam, port or starboard, you will not exactly be in an ideal position either as, depending on the wind strength, the boat will be pushed sideways away from the wind. This is known as 'leeway', a term accepted in everyday parlance but not often appreciated as being of nautical origin. However, the effect does have its uses as it can often blow you very neatly into an awkward space when mooring or conversely can be used to blow you out of one.

When moving ahead with a strong cross-wind care must be exercised in approaching bridges, locks or narrow channels. If you can, start upwind of the commencement of the restriction, so that by the time you reach it you are correctly placed.

Wind on your quarter (between the beam and the stern) will act rather like that on your bow but will tend to swing the vessel in the opposite direction. Wind on the port quarter will tend to swing your bow to port. Again – 'steer small' and always be ready to correct in plenty of time.

If the wind is coming from dead aft, steering will not be so impaired unless you allow the wind to wander on to either quarter, however, a strong wind will increase your speed in relation to your propeller speed so that manoeuvrability will possibly suffer, especially if you are required to take way off in an emergency.

Moving Astern. The wind effect on a hull moving astern differs from that affecting a stationary vessel or one moving ahead, in that the stern of a vessel moving astern tends to seek the wind. Since the rudder is less effective on a cruiser in reverse, a strong wind may tend to dictate completely the course followed. If you can, reverse so that you can make use of the wind, but note that the hull itself must have gathered way for the wind to be effective. Merely because your engines are in reverse does not mean that the stern will immediately swing to the wind. Propeller effects will count first as explained earlier. The Clerk of the Weather cannot follow the helmsman's actions on his gear lever.

HANDLING

Having now considered in detail the various forces and effects which come into play in the movement of our craft through the water we will proceed to detail some of the correct ways of solving various manoeuvring problems. Mooring and anchoring are dealt with in more detail in their respective sections of the manual, but before dealing with any manoeuvre which involves berthing, or leaving a quay or jetty we must learn the names and positions of the various mooring ropes. One or two uses of the anchor will also be discussed in so far as they affect the movement of our craft rather than its security when stopped in the river or in an anchorage. The main mooring ropes are shown in Fig. 15.

TURNING

In the section on the Rudder we discussed the effects of executing a turn, discounting considerations of wind and current. Remember the sequence when the helm is put over – 1. DRAG, slows you down, 2. CARRY; no immediate effect, the interval depending on hull design and the speed of the vessel, 3. SIDESLIP; away from the direction of turn, depending again on hull design and also size and position of the rudder, 4. The TURN, finally, on the pivot point of the vessel, normally a little forward of amidships. This means that the bow will swing in to take a small arc while the stern will swing out. Therefore, make sure that you have plenty of room. All round observation is essential at all times, especially when contemplating any manoeuvre described in this section.

Turning Short Round. When manoeuvring in restricted waters it is often desirable to turn the vessel through 180 degrees in as confined a space as possible. For inland cruisers of shallow draft there are two ways of doing this. For sea-going craft the second method is not as successful as the first, especially if the vessel has a pronounced vee-form hull or a substantial keel. Similarly a yacht under auxiliary power will be very difficult to turn in its own length by either method, but the first is the recommended one.

Put the helm to starboard and the engine ahead. As the swing gets going, engage reverse gear and open the throttle, bringing the helm amidships. The stern will now be paddled round by the sideways effect of the propeller which is running anti-clockwise. If you have chosen your location carefully in relation to the wind direction it will obviously be to your advantage to have your stern swinging into the wind at this point. Before way is gathered, reduce throttle and engage forward gear. Put helm over to starboard again. By now you may be right round so be prepared to meet the swing and check it by bringing the helm up to the 'bite' and checking that you do not swing too far. Easy! Practise it!

It may also be possible to turn virtually short round with a shallow draft cruiser in the opposite direction to that described above, due to the lack of a deep keel which, in sea-going craft, resists the turning action. In this case the reverse gear is not used. Put the helm hard a-port once the craft has stopped in the water and engage forward gear, running the engine at about quarter throttle. You MAY have to check making way by reversing for a short burst. If you do, reverse helm as well, i.e. put it hard a-starboard while the engine is running astern rather than leaving it amidships. Whichever way you go round you may find that a greater number of sequences of gear changing are required than are here described. This does not matter. The essence is to get the craft to turn in its own length and it is appreciated that the wind direction and current may dictate that a series of backing and filling is the only way to stop the craft moving out of position. If you can master the 'short round' turn none of the following manoeuvres should be difficult.

Always decide what you want to do first. Lay a plan of campaign, and if possible, tell the crew of what you intend, so that they can keep a sharp look-out. Be positive in your handling of the wheel but patient. Always remember that the rudder cannot act until the hull is moving through the water. Do not underestimate the sideways thrust of the propeller. Use it to your advantage and NEVER discount the effect of wind or current.

Three Point and Other Turns. Due to wind effects, it may not always be possible to turn short round, but, bearing in mind what effects the wind has on a ship, it is possible to make use of these, the primarily important one being that when moving astern the stern will always seek the wind, i.e. point up into the direction from which the wind is coming. The following pages are given over to six of the most usual cases.

Uses of Current in Turning. It was stated briefly, when we chatted about Current that the centre of the river, or the outside of a bend usually carries the strongest current, besides being deeper. The current against the bank is therefore comparatively sluggish. This factor can therefore be made use of to assist us in turning our craft. If the bow is put in towards the bank, the stronger current will carry the stern round and a complete change of direction effected without resorting to the use of the reverse gear.

If you are well acquainted with the river you may be aware of the composition of the river bed close to the bank, and if you know that it is of soft mud, you can allow the bow to 'bite' the mud temporarily. There is a famous mud bank opposite Yarmouth Yacht Station on the River Bure and when the tide ebbs the current runs out into Breydon Water at a fair speed. Boats coming downstream are always advised, if wishing to call at the Yacht Station to adopt this manoeuvre, to turn so that they can recross the river and moor correctly on the opposite side facing upstream. (See Broads Section).

LEAVING A BERTH

We assume that you are now familiar with the controls of your cruiser and once afloat and under way have a good idea of what and what not to do. You are, at the moment tied up alongside a quay by all or some of the ropes shown on Fig. 15. You are eager to start, but a little fearful, because every other holiday hirer who left the dock this morning has gone racing off in a most erratic manner, and has probably carved a lump of the quay off with his stern or a lump of his stern off with the quay. He has been roundly cursed by the lad on the petrol pumps and duly reported to the owners. Careful thought to the direction in which you are facing, in relation to wind and current and a solicitous enquiry as to which hand the propeller is and whether the gear shift is anything more complicated than forward for forward and back for reverse should set your mind at rest bearing in mind that we suggest you approach the manoeuvre of leaving a berth in one of the six following ways which cover the most

43

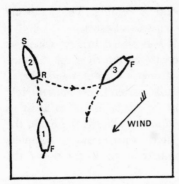

Fig. 16. Wind on bow

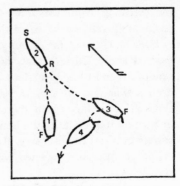

Fig. 17. Wind on quarter

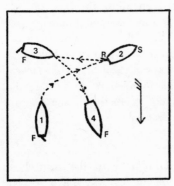

Fig. 18. Wind ahead

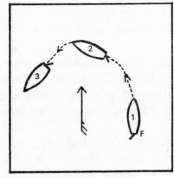

Fig. 19. Wind aft (astern)

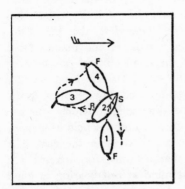

Fig. 20. Wind on port beam

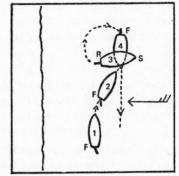

Fig. 21. Wind on starboard beam

usual predicaments in which you are likely to find yourself. If you are facing the wrong way, you might even try winding ship, i.e. turning it round in its berth without being unsecured from the quay. This is dealt with in the section on mooring, to which you should refer, if necessary. Remember, though, that it is strongly advocated that a cruiser should never be moored facing downstream, except in an estuary when the tide is flooding strongly, when to try and moor facing upstream would be very unwise.

Basic Principles. When leaving a berth, dock, quay, bank or from alongside other craft you MUST NOT FORGET that your craft swings on its axis. The stern will not therefore follow the track made by the bow. Get someone ashore or an agile member of your crew to watch the stern as you leave. Having let go your lines shove the bow off hard, and proceed with the helm amidships or slightly canted to allow for the athwartship thrust, if any, before the craft gathers way. Bring the helm over away from the bank gradually and you will be safely clear.

If it is not possible to shove off or such action will not cant you sufficiently because of wind and current, you can run a spring from your bow to the dock, level with the wheelhouse, say, and turn the helm into the dock, running engine ahead. This will bring the stern out into the stream. Take in the spring and reverse from the dock so that you have room to manoeuvre.

Conversely you can take a forespring from the stern to the dock, securing it level with the wheelhouse or amidships, put the helm over towards the dock or bank and run the engine astern. This will bring the bow out at which point you take in the spring and with helm amidships, go ahead.

If moored inside other craft, all of which are (and should be) facing upstream, let go their stern lines only and pass their bow-lines round your stem and secure these to the quay. Set up a backspring from your bow, and engage forward gear with the helm over towards the quay. Release your bow-rope and as soon as your own and the other craft have swung out, take in your back-spring and reverse out. The remaining craft can then be handled back in or driven in by the outside craft having its engine started and engaged in forward gear with the helm put over away from the dock.

You may probably have now realised that this swinging effect can be used to advantage in squaring craft up alongside. If the bow or stern is tethered then the whole craft will swing on these points depending on the position of the helm and the direction of propeller thrust. Forward thrust gives more positive results for reasons explained elsewhere in the manual. However, beware of getting the craft into a position where it is swung broadside on to the current, against the direction of such current, as the latter will often take over and what was a swing may turn into a broadside drift. If the angle of swing exceeds 45 degrees you may be approaching this condition and the only solution may be to cut the cruiser adrift. This is especially the case in crowded moorings where a strong stream is flowing.

Bearing these points in mind, we now described specific cases where these principles are brought into play with the added complication of wind and current effects.

Leaving a Berth (Case A). Facing Upstream – Wind Ahead or Astern – Port side to Quay. Start your engine. Let go your forward mooring lines. The current will now tend to push the bow out into the stream. Engage forward gear. Put the helm a quarter to half a turn of the wheel to starboard and run the engine to hold the boat in the current, edging slightly forward. Let go the stern lines, and maintain this position of helm and throttle until the vessel is well clear of the quay. Then increase speed. We are assuming in this case as in all described that your propeller is right handed (clockwise). The sideways thrust has therefore been paddling the stern away from the quay while the current has been pushing the bow out. If any craft are tied up ahead of you, you should be able to balance the propeller speed with the wind and current so that your vessel moves out sideways, making little or no headway at all as shown in Fig. 22.

Case B. As Case 'A' but Wind on Port Beam, Bow or Quarter. Execute this manoeuvre in exactly the same way but note that you will come out much faster since the wind will also assist you, especially if it is on the beam. If the wind is on the bow or the quarter, remember the turning effect that it will have upon your hull. If on the bow it will try to keep your stern in, therefore do not apply any starboard rudder and run the propeller a shade faster initially to offset the wind effect with the sideways thrust of the propeller. If on the quarter INCREASE starboard rudder to bring the bow out and there is no disgrace in getting a member of the crew to push off with the boat-hook. A brief note about the boat hook might be inserted here. For pushing off, it is better to use the blunt end. If the hook end slips, it can easily get caught in a ring or crack in the quay walling and either precipitate the crew into the water or left hanging to the shore while you are deftly moving away upstream.

Case C. As Case 'A' but with the Wind on the Starboard Beam, Bow or Quarter. This manoeuvre is more difficult, especially in a strong wind as it will tend to keep blowing you into the quay unless you think about it carefully. Remember to lay a plan of action first and then carry it out positively. With the wind on the bow it will probably be best to hold the boat on the forespring and forward breast rope, paying out the latter while the engine is run ahead with the helm to starboard. The bow will swing out and the stern, carefully fended by a member of the crew, will stick to the quay. When the wind is dead ahead bring both lines in, centre helm and proceed carefully ahead, away from the quay or bank. On the beam or quarter the best approach is to start the engine, engage gear and at a quarter throttle put the helm to port. Using the backspring only pay out the after breast so that the stern swings into the wind. Fend the bow carefully against the quay. Release both lines and bring the helm up to centre. Now reverse, the stern seeking the wind so that no further swing will take place until you are well clear of the quay. Square up to your course and go ahead when you are well clear, (Fig. 23).

Cases D, E, and F will be where the craft is facing upstream with the STARBOARD side of the craft to the quay or the bank. Remember that in all cases where a right handed propeller is involved on starting ahead the stern will be swung into the quay.

Case D. As Case 'A' but with a starboard quayside. In this case you will not be able to use the sideways thrust of the propeller to bring the stern out. Therefore, allow the bow to swing out until the wind is on the beam, if necessary, and then go slowly ahead, turning in midstream when clear. Do not execute a violent turn close to the quay or you will find your

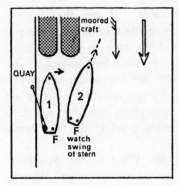

Fig. 22. Leaving quay to port. Wind ahead

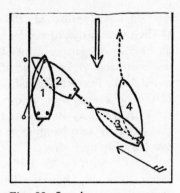

Fig. 23. Leaving quay to port. Wind abeam or on quarter

Fig. 24. Fitting out the dinghy for kedging off

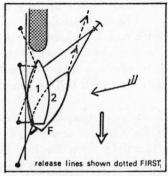

Fig. 25. Kedging off from quay

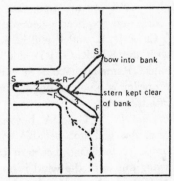

Fig. 26. Using a canal junction to turn round

stern clouting the quay as the vessel swings on her pivot point.

Case E. As Case 'B' but with the wind on the Starboard bow, beam or quarter with the quay to Starboard. If the wind is on the bow, treat this as Case 'D' except that a smaller swing will bring the wind on to your beam. If already on the beam, get your engine running ahead against the current slowly, then loose your lines and allow the wind to blow you clear. If on the quarter, it is best to swing the craft by means of current and propeller thrusting the stern against the quay so that the outward swing of the bow brings the wind dead aft. Then, releasing the stern rope and forespring last, go full ahead until well clear.

Case F. Wind on Port beam, bow or quarter with the quay to Starboard. With the wind on the bow or the beam hold the cruiser to the quay on the after breast rope and forespring and swing the cruiser by putting the engine ahead and helm to port until it has the wind dead ahead. Then, go forward, selecting your correct course when well clear. With the wind on the port quarter, proceed slowly ahead, leaving the backspring and forward breast rope secured. Put the helm to starboard and fend the bow. As soon as the stern is facing the wind, loose lines, centre helm and reverse the propeller. The cruiser will drop back stern to wind. When clear, put the helm to port, taking care that you are far enough from the quay not to be blown back onto it, engage forward gear and go ahead on course.

We are not considering mooring with the current astern as it is contrary to good practice. However, it may be necessary in tidal water to leave a berth with the tide astern if this has turned since berthing.

Start the engine but leave in neutral. Take in all lines except the backspring and aft breast rope which is eased while the helmsman puts the helm over away from the quay. The tide will ease the stern out and eventually the after breast rope is released. The engine is then put astern to ease the strain off the backspring, the helm put amidships and the backspring brought in as the craft moves away from the quay. When well clear the engine is put ahead and the correct course selected.

BERTHING OR COMING ALONGSIDE
The main consideration when berthing is to know how to stop.

Remember that very small but important paragraph in the Cruiser Controls section of the manual concerning the brakes. The basic principle of braking is that the only part of the vessel which will grip the water in which a vessel floats is the propeller. If drastic action is called for the anchor can be used. It is dealt with at the end of this section under 'Emergency Handling'. The propeller therefore has to serve as brake as well as driving force. If propelling a vessel forward, to stop it the propeller must be reversed or, if in reverse it must be put into forward drive. Having studied earlier sections you will realise that this is not as easy as it sounds, as once way is taken off a vessel she is not as easily manoeuvrable and wind, current and even propeller effects will come into play, causing the vessel to swing off course as soon as the braking effect is operative.

Let us assume you are travelling at 6 or 7 knots against a small current and there is little or no wind. You wish to stop. If you merely put the engine into reverse, the sideways thrust or 'paddle' effect of the propeller will tend to swing your stern to port (bow will appear to go to Starboard) and your rudder will become ineffective since the slipstream is now on the wrong side of the propeller. Incidentally this is mainly why a cruiser will not steer well in reverse. Do not try and correct the swing now. Your rudder will have no effect until you are actually making way astern, and that may prove as dangerous as going on ahead.

Since you have discovered, though, that your stern will swing, and precisely in which direction, the best way to complete the manoeuvre is to throttle down in plenty of time, come out of gear altogether, move the helm against the anticipated swing first and then engage gear to slow right up. The propeller effect, if your judgement on the helm was accurate should bring you back on course. It is virtually impossible to stop on the engines and helm alone in a dead straight line, but it is possible to compensate one swing with the other to finish on that line. With an experienced helmsman at the wheel the swings described would be very slight because knowledge of his ship will have taught him just when to compensate and by how much.

External effects can also be used to stop a cruiser. By turning head to wind and keeping it there with the throttle right back and finally disengaging gear, a vessel will stop, but remember that with way right off she will not be answerable to the helm and the tendency will be for her to sheer off and lie across the wind unless anchored or moored when stopped immediately. The most effective stopping method is to turn the vessel against the current, especially when berthing. With the engine running ahead against the current the craft will remain manoeuvrable until she is virtually stationary in relation to the quay. Lines should be taken ashore and secured as quickly as possible.

In any manoeuvre involving mooring, the engine should NEVER BE SWITCHED OFF until the Skipper is satisfied that his vessel is adequately secured. This may be stating the obvious but it is surprising how many knots unravel themselves immediately they are tied and also how many engines fail to restart within seconds of having been stopped.

Berthing – Case 1. Berthing to a Quay to Port – No wind or wind on Starboard beam. Approach the quay at an angle of about 30 degrees slowly against the current. When the bow is about fifteen feet or so off the quay, give the helm a quick turn to port to swing the bow in and then, centring helm, engage reverse and open the throttle. This will bring the stern in. If lines cannot yet be taken ashore, ease gear into forward and bring the helm to port again, repeating the sequence as above. Once the craft has stopped relative to the ground, if an onshore wind is blowing it will probably blow the craft in towards the quay. Make sure the side is well fended towards the quay and secure the head rope and forebreast first to stop the current taking the bow out again. Complete the mooring hitches to the requisite lines and then turn off the engine. If the craft is to be left for a long period unattended and there is a chance that the river level will rise or fall do not leave the breast ropes secure, as being short, they may break or cause damage if extra strain is applied to them through a change of level of the vessel in relation to the quay. This does not apply at pontoons.

Berthing – Case 2. As Case 1. but with wind on the Port Beam, i.e. an offshore wind. Approach quay at a slightly larger angle than in Case 1. (say 45 degrees) with the helm over towards the quay to prevent the bow blowing off too soon. When the bow is close in, smartly engage reverse, centring the helm to get the stern in. Do not do this too early or the bow will probably swing out again on the current. If someone is already ashore get them to catch a rope and secure the bow by the breast rope before attempting to bring the stern in.

Berthing – Case 3. As Case 1, but with wind ahead. Approach the quay at a fairly broad angle with the helm AWAY from the quay. This will bring the vessel into the wind and also reduce the angle until she is parallel with it. Centre helm, and give a short burst astern to take off way and bring the stern in. Get lines smartly ashore at the bow before the final swing catches the wind on the port bow and the vessel tries to pay off in the other direction.

Berthing – Case 4. As Case 1, but with wind astern. Steer towards the quay but keep parallel to it and a little way off, roughly the vessel's width and a half. When two lengths from the actual position at which you are required to moor, turn the wheel towards the quay and let the bow approach. Just short of the quay, centre helm and reverse to bring the stern in. In this case it may be advantageous to overshoot the mooring slightly and allow the vessel to gather way astern. The wind will then be able to check any further swing.

Berthing – Cases 5, 6, 7 & 8. These cases follow the first four but are to a Starboard quay. The reverse sideways thrust of the propeller cannot therefore be used for both stopping way and swinging the stern in. Finer angles of approach must therefore be used (about half the angles quoted above). If the reverse gear has to be used to take way off, do this earlier, well out from the quay. If you do arrive too fast and a stern swing is started which will damage the vessel or quay, reverse helm and back off with the current and try again. Once the bow is secured a touch AHEAD on the engine will bring the stern in. The four cases will not therefore be detailed individually.

USING THE ANCHOR

Apart from anchoring a ship at rest, the anchor, which is discussed more fully in its own section can be used in situations where turns or getting under way are not possible without its assistance.

Turning on the Anchor. This may be necessary where a strong current is flowing and the execution of a short round turn may be dangerous in that the current will have set you into other moored craft or fixed obstacles by the time the turn is completed. To help maintain your position in relation to the ground a temporary hold to the river bed is advisable. If a turn with the current as described previously is considered too risky owing to the speed of the flow and one is proceeding upstream it will be necessary to use the 'kedge' anchor from the stern. If turning to port the anchor MUST be streamed from the starboard quarter, otherwise the chain will foul the propeller. This would be the normal way to turn in these conditions anyway, since turning in the opposite direction would involve crossing to the 'wrong' side of the channel.

Close with the bank (to starboard) and steam ahead, letting go the kedge anchor from the starboard quarter and pay out enough chain to allow the anchor to 'bite'. Turn the helm to port, still going ahead. Slight drag of the anchor is permissible. The bow will now be approaching the centre of the stream where the current is stronger and will tend to swing, since the stern is held back by the anchor which has been dropped in slower moving water. As the turn is completed it will now be necessary to raise the anchor. The chain will now be under strain with the anchor upstream from the vessel. Ease the strain by reversing between the anchor position and the bank. At no time should the chain be allowed to grow across the axis of the craft or risk of fouling the propeller or rudder will be present. Get the anchor in and then resume course. Do not try and raise the anchor while moving forward and on no account try to bring it aboard over the stern. IT MUST come up over the quarter or even further forward to ensure it is clear of the propeller.

If a turn is contemplated with a strong wind or stream astern, the anchor may again be used by turning the *bow* into the bank as described under 'Use of Current in Turning' as mentioned above.* Let go the anchor on the windward or upstream side of the vessel and allow it to bite while the stronger stream takes the stern round. If a stern wind is the cause dictating the manoeuvre the helm should be put over to the side the anchor has been dropped and power ahead maintained. Under these conditions remember when retrieving the anchor it

* See page 43.

is imperative to reverse off the anchor chain so that it grows (leads away from the vessel) ahead. Letting it grow under the bow will mean that the flukes will probably damage the topsides when it is brought aboard.

Getting away from a Berth with the Anchor. If the wind is blowing strongly onshore it may not be possible to get a vessel away from her berth without the assistance of the kedge. The separate kedge anchor may be supplied with the craft. A well equipped vessel will always have one. The kedge can also be used in conjunction with the main anchor for holding the ship's head to a tighter circle when anchored in a tideway than a single anchor allows. (See Anchor Section). In this case it is used for its old purpose in the days of sail when it was carried ahead of the ship in the longboat and dropped on a long warp so that by winching in, the ship would be slowly hauled forward when becalmed. Known as 'kedging off' the procedure is as follows :

Coil the kedge warp on the thwarts of the dinghy and place the anchor, flukes uppermost, over the stern with a loop round the shank, taken from a point either side of the dinghy amidships. Make sure that the warp is securely fastened to the anchor ring (or chain, if one is provided) and leads from the anchor to the bottom of the coil. Now row out into the stream, paying out the line to the cruiser from the top of the coil where the standing end of the warp is attached via the hawsepipe to the winch and cleat or chain locker fastening. When positioned upstream at a reasonable distance from the cruiser, let go the kedge by releasing the loop. Return to the cruiser and commence hauling on the kedge warp, releasing the forward mooring lines. The cruiser will now begin to ride towards the kedge anchor. Start the engine and when clear of the quay proceed ahead inside the kedge so that the warp does not cross the bow. Winch kedge clear and bring aboard. (Figs. 24 & 25.)

A word of warning. Do not try taking the kedge out IN the dinghy. You will probably get a ducking, trying to heave it over the side when you arrive at your destination in midstream.

CANALS

Handling of all types of cruiser differs in many respects on canals to river or estuary, the difference deriving mainly from the confined nature of canals, both in width and depth. A cruiser that draws anywhere near the maximum permissible draft on the waterway in question will not be able to navigate far from the main channel.

CURRENT EFFECTS

The largest bugbear to be contended with is silting, which occurs more easily now that power craft are by far the largest canal users and the days of the horse-drawn narrow boat are nearly over. A slight amount of current in a canal may be noticed, where the British Waterways Board have sold pumping rights to local water boards, who extract the canal water for local supply purposes to the canal hinterland.

At locks, the current may increase due to lock working, and many locks possess by-pass weirs which will also cause a set in the direction of the weir which should be negotiated accordingly. The remarks applicable to current effects earlier in this section are, of course, also relevant to canal craft.

WIND EFFECTS

Shallow draught boats such as canal-cruisers are especially prone to the effects of the wind. In high winds, on exposed sections of canal it is often easier and distinctly advisable to moor up in a gale or strong breeze than to try to navigate the cut by continually fending off from the bank, only to be blown back on to it again.

SPEED

Ignoring for the moment the speed limits laid down in the bye-laws, you must remember that every boat has an optimum speed, at which its engine works best in relation to the hull design and also the depth and width of the channel in which it is navigated. In any canal, especially of the narrow variety (having locks of approximately 7 feet wide) the boat's speed will probably be solely dictated by its hull's ability to allow water to flow under its keel.

To find this optimum speed, advance the throttle and then start easing it back until you notice a drop in speed of the craft. Excessive speed will cause considerable wash and damage to the banks of the cut, and will also tend to lower the stern increasing the risk of damage to the propeller on the bottom. It may be possible to vary the speed according to the state of the canal, but you should always reduce speed at restrictions, such as bridge-holes, tunnels and aqueducts where silting or debris may be more prevalent.

TURNING EFFECT

Earlier in this section we discussed the pivot point of our average river cruiser. The pivot point on a narrow boat conversion, however, is usually to be found much further back and this will mean that the bow of such a cruiser will tend to swing widely when the helm is applied. The pivot point on such craft is usually related to the weight distribution in the hull, and since the engine is usually mounted well aft the pivot point will be just forward of the engine. In the vessel shown in Fig. 8 it would be in the centre of the hull about level with the aft 2-tier bunks.

You should always turn a narrow boat in a basin or in the winding holes provided, if you wish to turn round completely. Elsewhere in the cut, the channel may look wide enough, but due to heavy silting at the banks you may end up jammed across the cut, a predicament which will spoil your holiday and make you extremely unpopular with other users of the canal.

Turning, by backing and filling can also be executed at canal junctions as shown in Fig. 26 provided you will not be obstructing other craft and that you have made sure in advance that it is safe for you to do so. Bring the bow close to the bank away from the junction and swing the stern into a position from which you can reverse up the branch canal. Then go forward, making sure that you do not cut the corner too closely as you rejoin the main stream. For clarity, the diagram excludes any locks or bridges, a bridge often being positioned across the entrance to the canal arm so that the towpath of the main line can be continued from bank to bank. You should therefore note that such a bridge will provide an obstruction to your line of sight from the main line and a crew member should be posted ashore to ascertain that the arm is clear, before commencing your turn.

NOTES ON TWIN SCREW VESSELS

Certain small craft are sometimes fitted with twin engines having twin propellers, offset equidistant from the centre-line of the vessel on either side of a central rudder, or having individual rudders placed in their slipstreams. Run together the propellers will not therefore have any sideways effect as they are usually 'handed' (i.e. they turn in opposite directions when in the same gear), neither is there likely to be any propeller race effect since equal forces are applied to the opposite sides of each rudder. The 'handing' is usually arranged so that the port engine when run ahead turns in an anti-clockwise direction while the starboard engine turns in a clockwise direction.

There are certain disadvantages in twin screw installations in small craft relating to engine siting and weight. The question of reliability, probably brought into doubt by skimped servicing due to restrictions of space also must not be overlooked. Such installations are, however, not uncommon in quite small craft, built for an indulgent owner, or where considerations of handling apply.

Generally speaking, a twin screw vessel is easier to handle for reasons which will become apparent in these notes. The basic principle relied on and the one factor which dictates installation design is that since the propellers are offset, one or the other run on its own or faster than its counterpart will assist in turning the craft. With the port propeller stopped and the starboard propeller run ahead the vessel will turn to port, even though the rudder is set amidships. It follows that if the port engine is put into reverse gear the swing will be stronger and if run slowly ahead, the swing weaker.

Where an adverse wind is trying to blow the head off, say to starboard, the starboard engine can be run a shade faster than the port engine so that correcting helm, tiresome to the helmsman and causing drag on the hull can be eliminated. The rule can therefore be formulated as : Run the leeward engine faster than the windward one where the wind is ahead of the beam,

57

the windward engine faster where the wind is abaft the beam (i.e. on the quarter).

TURNS
It is possible to turn short round in either direction by running the engine inside the turn in reverse, the outer at similar speed ahead. If way is made during the manoeuvre in either direction REDUCE the speed of the corresponding engine (the engine propelling in the direction of craft movement) or bring it into neutral momentarily altogether.

We airily remarked that the sideways propeller effect does not apply to a twin-screw vessel. Some authorities may care to argue the point but, remembering our study of sideways effects on single engined craft we learned that a standard clockwise installation, when run ahead, paddles the stern to starboard. Its degree of effect is dictated mainly by propeller size. The starboard propeller of a twin screw vessel also turns clockwise and MAY paddle the stern to starboard but remember it is smaller, being only half of the driving force available and it is therefore doubtful if this effect is as important as the one of its being offset, which swings the bow to port anyway. For this reason the sideways effect can be ignored in twin-screw vessel handling theory.

For fuller details of manoeuvring twin screw vessels you are strongly recommended to 'Little Ship Handling : Motor Vessels' by Lt. Cmdr. M. J. Rantzen, R.N.V.R., published by Herbert Jenkins.

EMERGENCY HANDLING

STRANDING
One is guilty of stranding, but beaching is a deliberate act on the part of the master of a vessel. In everyday parlance on the waterways we term it with less politeness and refer to it as 'running aground' with a flippancy which it does not deserve, because it never happens to us by accident, and we never do it deliberately because we know how awkward it can be to get afloat again.

If you go aground *STOP THE ENGINE IMMEDI-ATELY*!!! Check that the water circulation system is clear by opening the strainer stand-pipes and withdrawing the filters, having CLOSED any necessary sea-cocks. If clear, try reversing. If the bow is stranded, bring as much weight aft to lift it and go astern. Do not forget that a bow fitted water tank contains water weighing 10 lb. per gallon, so that emptying of such a tank can help considerably. If still fast, bring the weight *forward* to reduce the area of hull in contact with the river bed and then reverse. If an inspection of the strainers reveals that the inlets are covered by mud and/or weed the engine should not be re-started until the vessel has been moved into clearer water so that the following methods suggested should also include the above procedure, whether it has been decided that reverse propeller could refloat the craft or not.

It may be possible to lever the cruiser off the mud by going over the side and heaving on improvised crowbars, utilising the mooring irons etc,. Don't use the boat-hook! You will probably snap it. Apply any pressure to the hull via a fender. Wood and G.R.P. hulls do not take kindly to cold steel and any strain should be taken slowly and evenly, keeping a careful watch on the hull form itself.

Putting a kedge out into deeper water from the stern and hauling off on that in a similar manner to that described on pages 53 and 124 may be successful. If in weed, make sure that the propeller is cleared, as are the cooling water inlets before starting the engine again.

IF PERMANENTLY AGROUND, INFORM THE WATERWAY AUTHORITY AT ONCE.

WEED

If weed is suspected round the propeller, often indicated by sluggish propulsion at normal revs. or 'lumpy' running, stop the propeller by disengaging the gear and give it quick short bursts in reverse. A member of the crew should be posted at the stern to watch the surge of water under the transome, as any weed will be thrown up if cleared. Failing this, in clearer water it may be possible to pull the weed off carefully with the boat-hook, from the bank or the dinghy. If you have run through loose weed, check the strainers as soon as convenient and pass the deck mop over the water inlets to clear away any weed which may have caught across the inlet.

Canal cruisers are often provided with a weed trap over the propeller which consists of a well in the hull and a stout hatch cover which can be removed so that easy access can be gained from the cockpit or steering position above to the propeller, should it become entangled with weed or rubbish thrown up from the bed of the canal.

Incidentally, 'lumpy' running referred to above is often an indication that the hull is close to, if not on, the bottom. In such cases, shut down the throttle. It means that you are probably going too fast. REDUCED SPEED WILL RAISE THE STERN and thus assist you. To try and thrash on, regardless, may eventually stop you altogether and make matters worse if you are a little behind schedule.

IF ANY ATTENTION HAS TO BE GIVEN TO THE PROPELLER OR WATER INLETS MAKE CERTAIN THAT THE ENGINE CANNOT BE TURNED. HIDE THE CRANK HANDLE, REMOVE THE KEY, or DISCONNECT THE BATTERY.

The authors' personal preference is to carry out the latter precaution. Some diesel cruisers do not possess a key.

ENGINE STALL

If the engine stalls – DROP THE ANCHOR *IMMEDIATELY*! Therefore *ALWAYS* have the anchor shackled to its chain. If in midstream it is imperative to get out of the way of other shipping. When the anchor is down, pull in or let out chain, so that the anchor drags slightly. Check the best bank for mooring, bearing in mind that it is preferable to have dropped the anchor from the bow away from the bank. Put the helm towards the bank as soon as the craft has settled down to face upstream or head to tide. The stern will now swing towards the bank selected and the bow and anchor will follow as the anchor drags. It is best, when 'dredging' as this manoeuvre is called, to PORT to have the anchor chain let go from the starboard hawsepipe or fairlead or vice versa as explained above. In this way, the anchor chain will not damage your topsides.

If the engine stalls on a canal, steer for the bank. Avoid

using your anchor on any canal, especially under such circumstances.

MAN OVERBOARD DRILL
This is dealt with in a separate section of the manual (q.v.).

ROPE FOULED IN PROPELLER
This is becoming a common fault with many hire cruiser customers, and is of extreme annoyance to them and the owners, because the cost of removing the rope is usually borne by the customer and the chore of removing it is reserved by the owner. Some enlightened owners, however, offer succinct advice over the telephone as to how it can be done to save themselves the trouble of stirring far from their yard, but if you are a hirer, it is better to telephone your parent yard than try and take unauthorised action for fear of losing your precious deposit.

To the private owner, however, who may save himself a bit of time and money by attempting the job himself here is our advice for what it is worth, but first let us explore the prevention rather than the cure.

The first important thing is to make sure that your backspring, forebreast and headrope are too short to reach the propeller anyway. Secondly, it helps to use a polypropylene rope, since, in theory, this floats if dropped in the water.

Under these conditions, therefore, the most likely occasion when a rope will be caught up in the prop is when you are entering a lock or coming alongside a landing stage or quay. Your man at the stern chucks the rope at a likely looking assistant lock-keeper (chief lock-keepers never miss catching a rope!), he drops it and the whole horrible fankle splashes into the water just by the stern at the very moment when the helmsman is running the prop at top revs. in reverse to try and slow the boat up.

As described elsewhere in this manual, our usual procedure in such circumstances is to holler 'PROPS' at which the sufficiently schooled helmsman shuts the gear into neutral. If the line is still attached to the stern cleats, start to haul it in until it goes taut. Turn off the engine and leave the stop knob on a diesel out (i.e. so that the engine cannot fire) or switch the ignition off on a petrol engine (for a similar result). Still holding your line firmly pull it out by the quarter, about level with the propeller shaft exit from the skeg and press the starter button. The prop will slowly revolve with the gear engaged in forward drive, and with luck, the line will unwind itself from the shaft.

If it does not, try the next line of approach. Locate the gear box/propeller shaft coupling flange, which is usually mounted close to the rear end of the gear box and consists of two flanges bolted together by means of four bolts. Undo the bolts and slide the prop shaft towards the stern. There is usually some distance between the flange and the stern greaser which is positioned at the head of the sterntube for this to be done. Your propeller is now, therefore, some inches clear of the point where the tube in the skeg ends and will revolve in either direction required by the method in which the rope has wound itself up. The rope should now come off fairly easily and with a bit of patience will even unwrap itself from any propeller blades with which it has got caught up.

Failing either of these two methods, it is probably best to don swimming trunks and go over the side to the job. However, if you do elect to try this, make sure that the battery is disconnected from the engine circuits so that no one, however foolish can mash your hand off by inadvertently turning the engine by means of the starter. The job is probably easier done anyway by disconnecting the coupling flange as the prop will turn more readily if disengaged from the gear box.

LOCKS

General
How a Lock Works
Half-Locks
Using the Locks
Manned Locks
Manual Operation of Hydraulic Locks
Unmanned Lock Working
Using Unmanned Locks
Lock Drill
Side Ponds
Lock Flights and Staircases
Staircase Variations
Lock Troubles and Simple Cures
Guillotine Gates
Guard Locks

Illustrations

63

SECTION IV

LOCKS AND LOCK-WORKING

GENERAL

On the Thames, Trent and Severn, all locks are manned by keepers. On other waterways, including some of those still in commercial use this is not generally the case, and it may be found by the more venturesome enthusiast that he will therefore be required to work a lock for himself. This section therefore discusses the various procedures for lock-working, both manned and unmanned with an introduction for the unenlightened on the basic reasons for locks and the principles that underlie their working.

There are no operable locks on the Broads except for the Oulton Lock into Lowestoft Harbour (Lake Lothing) which is manned. This lock has double gates, since both sides are affected by differing tides and the lock has therefore been constructed to work either way.

The reason for locks on canals is probably self-evident, since artificially constructed waterways are obliged to change level as the canal-planner has to take into account the route and distance of the watercourse irrespective, to some degree, of the geography that lies between the two points on the map he wishes to link. In certain cases this can be overcome by excavation, tunnelling and embanking, but excessive costs are involved in such undertakings compared with lock construction.

The reason for a lock on a river, however, may not be so immediately apparent, but it will be realised that boating would be almost impossible if the current was allowed to flow unchecked from source to estuary, especially in times of wet weather when serious flooding, especially in the lower reaches could occur. In dry weather the level might fall so much, even leaving the upper reaches dry, that navigation would be impossible because the depth of water was insufficient. To check the flow and retain a depth sufficient for navigation, artificial dams or 'weirs' are constructed, thus dividing the river up into several levels or 'steps'. In order to step up or down, a boat must therefore make use of a lock, in which the water level in which it floats is raised or lowered so that it can proceed on the next section. The modern lock of the type found on the Thames below Oxford and on the Trent below Nottingham, is now electrically operated, in some cases from a central cabin on the lockside.

HOW A LOCK WORKS
The basic lock has two sets of gates at either end of a chamber which is normally rectangular in plan. Diamond shaped and circular locks are a rarity but exist in one or two cases, especially on the canals. The top gates hold back the water at the upper level (in the case of a river – at the upstream end), the level being dictated by the adjacent weir and amount of flow of the river or canal (where applicable). The bottom gates hold the water at this high level only so that the top gates can be opened to permit the passage of craft into or out of the lock from the higher level.

Sluices or paddles (in the North, termed cloughs, pronounced 'clows') are provided, either at the base of the gates (gate paddles) or in the lock side (ground paddles) to permit the lock to be filled or emptied so that the levels of water in the lock can be equated, either with the upstream or downstream sides. If the lock is empty only the lower gates can be moved – if full only the top gates can be moved. A slight difference in level is sufficient to prevent movement of the gates owing to the water pressure. To meet this pressure the gates, in plan, represent a 'V', the point of the 'V' being directed upstream or towards the higher level. Variations of this arrangement are quite common especially on the narrow canals where single or 'clapper' gates are found, usually on the upstream end of a lock, forming the top gate. A further variation on one or two canals and extensively on the Fenland rivers is the guillotine gate which consists of a wood or steel shutter which rises and falls in guides set in the lockside and operated by overhead lifting gear.

Craft proceeding upstream enter by the bottom gates into the empty lock. The gates are shut and the lower sluices closed. The sluices at the upper, or top gates are opened and the lock fills to the level of the river beyond the top gates. The gates are opened and the craft proceed out of the lock. In the return direction, if the lock is empty, the bottom gate sluices are closed, the top gate sluices opened and the lock fills to the level of the upper river or canal. The top gates can then be opened, craft proceed into the lock and the top gates and sluices are closed. The bottom gate sluices are opened, the lock empties and the bottom gates opened to allow the craft to proceed downstream or on to the lower section of canal.

HALF-LOCKS
On the Thames and other waterways catering for small craft, at times of drought it is often necessary to conserve water. In this case half the lock length can be used by operating a central pair of gates which, under normal conditions, are left open. In this way only half the usual volume of water is used. When in use the lower or upper half of the lock is not used, the top or bottom gates being left open and the half-lock gates acting as one or other set of gates.

USING THE LOCKS
When navigating any waterway it is essential to have a good map or guide showing the positions of the locks in relation to

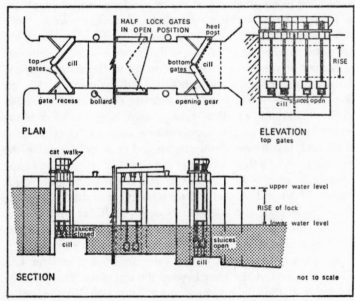

Fig. 27. A hydraulically operated lock (R. Thames)

66

their attendant weirs. Always give a weir a wide berth, whether you are above or below it. Above a weir there is a strong current which may not be apparent on the water's surface; below it there will be strong cross- and under-currents and possible silting to say nothing of the seething surface water. In some cases there may be submerged piles or breakwaters which divide the lock channel from the weir stream to add to the general hazards. By-pass weirs exist on many canals, to avoid excessive pound levels pouring over the top of lock-gates, so that these remarks should certainly not be ignored by the canal user.

Approach and enter locks slowly but NOT so slowly that you lose steerage way and control of your craft.

MANNED LOCKS

If, on approach, the gates are closed against you, moor to the bank or piles provided, generally to the right (correct) side of the gates. If no mooring piles are provided, moor to the bank well clear of the lock entrance. Remember, as soon as the gates open craft may be coming out of the lock and in any event the water below the gates will be considerably disturbed by the sluices emptying the lock if you are waiting at the lower level. If at the upper level, waiting to descend you will be in a better position to see what is going on in the lock as the craft using the lock will come into view over the tops of the gates before they are opened.

When cleared or signalled to do so by the lock-keeper, enter the lock carefully. Make allowances for windage on your boat and any cross current from the weir stream. Station the crew at convenient points with fenders to prevent damage to the cruiser's top sides as she moves in. Fenders should be used and watched while the whole locking process is under way. Do not dash into a lock and then reverse, flinging warps all over the place to stop your craft. You will probably damage it if you do. Take the bow warp ashore first and see that it is secure round a bollard, preferably held by a member of the crew on the tug-boat or 'Thames' hitch shown on Fig. 43. To tuck the stern in bring the helm away from the lock's side at which the bow warp is held and engage forward gear, or if practicable use the athwartship thrust of the propeller.

Do not moor close to the top gates since these are protected by a cill below the surface, although in some cases the cill can be easily seen when the lock is empty. On the Thames where the cill is not visible the extent of it is denoted either by a white line painted up the side of the lock or a plate in the lock wall which reads: 'NO MOORING ABOVE THIS POINT'. When locking down it is particularly important to position your craft properly. If placed too far back in the lock your sterngear will settle on the cill which will cause expensive damage as the water runs out of the lock. Moored too close to the bottom gates, you may hit them when the level drops as soon as the sluices are drawn as such action tends to draw craft in that direction. It is therefore essential to be correctly positioned and to have your lines tended (NEVER *TIED*) at the bollards provided. NEVER make fast to a bollard in a lock. The best method is to take the line ashore, round the bollard and back on board again. This will obviate the difficulty of getting a crew member back on board in a deep lock when locking down. If going up, it is therefore wise, before entering a deep lock to post a member ashore before the lock so that he can meet you at the lock and take your lines ashore and pass them back to you. He can rejoin the craft when the level has risen sufficiently for him to board with ease.

Once in position in a manned lock, it is courteous to switch off the engine and also any radio. You may miss the lock-keeper's instructions to you if you don't. On the Thames, you are particularly requested to follow this rule. It is also a rule, based on safety precautions that matches or lighters should not be lit in a lock owing to the fire hazard present with 'Calor' gas and petrol vapour in confined surroundings. You may possibly be sharing the lock with other craft and a fire or explosion would be a very serious matter indeed.

As the sluices are operated make sure that in ascending you do not move too far forward. An undertow is set up which pitches the craft forward when locking up and collision with the top gates could be a serious matter. It is not unknown for the prow of a vessel to get lodged under the gate rails in such circumstances which will damage the gates and may also eventually waterlog your craft.

To leave the lock, start your engine as soon as the gate

forward begins to open. Bring all lines aboard and instruct the crew to tend the fenders as the cruiser moves forward. Projecting piles and rubbing strakes in a lock can rip fenders off quite easily if they are not carefully supervised. A crew member should always be ready with the boat-hook (blunt end for preference) to fend off the lock-side as, since you will have little way on, the cruiser may not answer readily to the helm at first. Do not accelerate until well clear. Damage is caused to gates and sluices by unnecessary revving of the propellers. Your courtesy will always be noted by any lock-keeper or waterway official and appreciated.

MANUAL OPERATION OF HYDRAULIC LOCKS (THAMES)

The Thames locks below Oxford are mechancially or hydraulically operated by means of electrical control gear, which is switched off when the lock-keeper is not on duty. Lock-keepers are devoted men and it is not often that you will be let down by them, but they must eat from time to time and in the summer they cannot be expected to work right through until very late in the evening. It may be that for urgent reasons you require to use the lock, and after all, the river is just as much a highway as the road and you cannot therefore be prevented from passing through the locks. The following notes are quoted from the current edition of the Thames Conservancy Launch Digest, which you will do well to obtain. It costs you nothing but a request to the Conservancy for a copy.

'There are electro-mechanical locks at Mapledurham and Cookham with separate hand operation for lock gates and sluices which may be opened or closed in a normal manner by turning the appropriate handles.

'All other mechanical locks are power-operated by electro-hydraulic mechanism and the procedure for hand operation is as follows :

1. Ensure that both pairs of lock gates are properly closed.

2. Fill the lock as necessary by lowering the selector lever (on the left of the operating pedestal) to 'Sluice' position and rotating the handwheel (clockwise) to open or (anti-clockwise) to close the sluices.

3. When water levels are correct raise the selector lever to

'Gate' position and rotate the handwheel (clockwise to open or anti-clockwise) to close the gates.

Hand operation of mechanical locks is necessarily slow.

Please leave the lock empty with the gates closed.'

Teddington and Molesey Locks are open 24 hours a day, i.e. lock staff are permanently in attendance.

Manual locks may also be worked by the public under the circumstances described above. Gate opening and closing provides more than a little light exercise and the sluice operation is in many cases by means of counterbalanced wheel gear as shown in the accompanying figure. When the red-tipped shaft is uppermost the sluice is open. (Fig. 28).

On other waterways you will probably find that the public are expressly forbidden to operate lock and sluice gear at manned locks. Navigation is therefore restricted to the hours of duty of the lock staff which should be ascertained before passage is contemplated.

UNMANNED LOCK WORKING INCLUDING RIVERS AND WATERWAYS WITH BROAD LOCKS

The broad canals are defined as those capable of carrying craft having a beam wider than seven feet, which is the standard beam width of the conventional narrow boat. Thus the widths vary between canal and canal. The Grand Union Canal has locks 14 feet wide and some waterways vary to more than this but most are less. For example, the River Nene which runs from Northampton to the Wash starts with a beam width of 13 feet running up to 20 feet at the Dog-in-a-Doublet Lock just beyond Peterborough.

The sluices or 'paddles' are connected by rods which travel up the face of the gate to racks which are raised or lowered by pinions which are driven by means of gears from a shaft which is carried along the balance beam to a dog or 'key' on which the lock windlass can be fitted by the operator. Alternatively, or in addition, ground sluices may be provided. These consist of culverts running from the pound above the lock and discharging in the lock itself beyond the cill. The paddle is set in the culvert and is raised and lowered by a similar type of rack and pinion arrangement which comes up through the stonework on the lockside close to the top gate. Ground sluices at bottom gates are not common. Figs. 29 and 30 show typical examples of sluice winding gear with the parts named with which we are concerned. Ground and gate paddle gear are usually provided with a pawl and ratchet, so that the pawl can be dropped when the rack is in the raised (paddle 'open') position and the windlass removed to operate another sluice.

Windlasses are usually provided by hire yards against a small deposit. For most B.W.B. canals windlasses can be hired from the Board, and application should be made to the Pleasure Craft Licensing Officer, Willow Grange, Church Road, Watford, Herts. Private owners may of course, wish to purchase these, and details of the engineering firms which market them can be obtained from the Inland Waterways Association Ltd., 114, Regents Park Road, London, N.W.1.

YOU ARE WARNED, however, that in the Fens the Welland and Nene River Authority advise that the lifting gates and the paddles on the mitre gates are normally locked and that lock keys should be obtained from the Engineer's office at North Street, Oundle (Tel: Oundle 3366). The control gear is operated by a windlass to fit a $1\frac{1}{4}$ in. shaft. Windlasses are NOT SUPPLIED by the Authority. On the Great Ouse from Tempsford to St Ives lock handles ARE supplied by the Great Ouse River Authority on loan for a small annual charge and

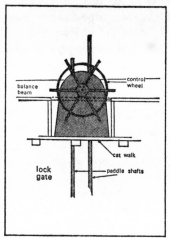

Fig. 28. River Thames manual sluice control gear

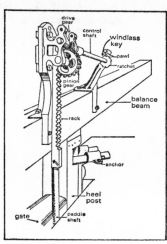

Fig. 29. Gate paddle gear

71

subject to the signing of an agreement as to their use. 'Home-made' or handles not issued by the Authority are forbidden. Contravention of this rule may invoke a claim for heavy damages and may also prejudice the free use of the river for all other boating people. Paddles, in Fen country are usually referred to as 'slackers'.

If a B.W.B. lock is chained and padlocked, however, this indicates that the gates so secured should not be used. Prior information as to the closure of the lock is normally available from Watford (address above) or from the Board's staff on the waterway in question. Do not hesitate, ever, to approach water-way officials for information of this kind, and discuss with them your proposed route so that they can advise you of any peculiarities of your itinerary. They are also a mine of informa-tion on moorings, pubs and shops if you are in strange country, although much of this information is contained in the Canals Book or Fens Book, each of which is published every year and is excellent value at 7s. 6d. from most bookshops. The British Waterways Board also publish excellent booklets containing line information on the more popular canals.

USING THE LOCKS (UNMANNED)

The method of approach to a lock is already explained earlier in this section. However, it should be borne in mind that, with no lock staff to assist you, it will be easier to post one or more members of the crew ashore, well before the lock so that they can go on ahead to prepare the lock if necessary prior to your entry. If the lock is already in use, they can signal the position to your helmsman in plenty of time. Indeed, many crew mem-bers have been known never to get a trip afloat as they spend their time 'lock-wheeling', that is riding along the towpath on a bicycle from lock to lock making each one ready and then shutting the paddles and gates after the vessel has gone through. Where locks are close together, this practice saves a lot of time.

Do not forget that many locks have by-pass weirs, the current from which must be allowed for when entering or leaving a lock, both above it and below. Narrow boats are also sensitive to wind and in narrow locks will have only inches to spare. Where any craft is going to be a tight fit in the lock, particularly the narrow boat of 70 feet length, the best practice is to bring the bow up to the entrance of the lock fairly gently. Remember, though that an excessively slow speed will give you little steerage way and on a long hull with the pivot point well aft, a small adjustment of the tiller will be magnified into quite a wide swing of the bow.

Once the cheeks of the bow are held by the lock entrance, suitably fended, of course, use the sideways thrust of the propeller or the helm and engine to line the rest of the hull up with the lock chamber and then engage forward gear to get her in. In a broad lock, take the lines ashore as previously described, but in a narrow lock it is perhaps better to dispense with the lines which are probably unnecessary and control the position of the craft by means of the engine. Let the bow just touch the top cill when locking up and keep engine ticking over in forward gear so as to keep the stern off the the bottom gates. As the level rises, be prepared to engage reverse to ease the craft off the top gates as she clears the cill. A touch on the throttle should do the trick.

Conversely when, locking down go well down the lock to the bottom gates so that the sterngear clears the cill. You may start to run back, so give a touch ahead to correct this.

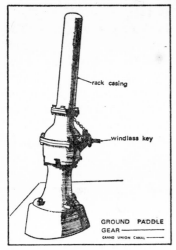

Fig. 30. Ground paddle gear (Grand Union Canal)

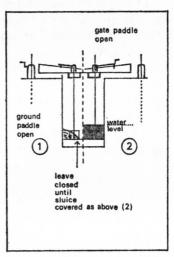

Fig. 35. Top gate paddle sequence

In broad locks, it is better to rely on line-handling for keeping your position as use of the engine may swing you across the lock. The boat-hook is also useful here for keeping you in position by fending the opposite wall. If you open the ground paddle on the same side as your craft first, this will also help to keep you in.

LOCK-DRILL
The standard lock drill given here is that which has been evolved over a number of years by the British Waterways Board and their predecessors. Leaflets are issued to describe it. It is simple and straightforward and more than anything is based on the common-sense solution to the problem of lock-working. There are no frills or hidden arts for you to worry about.

Figures 31 and 32 deal with the ascent of a lock from the lower to upper levels, figures 33 and 34 with the descent. In both cases in these figures, it is assumed that the lock is against you as you approach, i.e. that the lock is full when you wish to ascend and that it is empty when you wish to descend. If the lock is found to be with you when you approach e.g. it is empty when you wish to ascend, then follow the diagrams in each case from DIAGRAM 'B', or 'F', respectively.

The majority of locks are provided with ground sluices at the upper gates. ALWAYS OPERATE THE GROUND SLUICE GEAR FIRST before attempting to raise the gate paddles. The reason for this, especially in narrow locks, is that the gate paddles are usually much higher than the ground sluice outlets and that to open these into an empty lock containing a sizeable craft will often cause extreme turbulence in the lock and where a narrow boat has its bow right up against the cill can easily fill the boat, rather than the lock!

The official recommendation is that the gate paddles should not be 'drawn' (raised) until the lock is two-thirds full, although in practice they are usually drawn as soon as they are covered by the water level attained by drawing the ground paddles, as shown in Fig. 35.

GOING UPHILL (ASCENDING) – LOCK FULL
1. See that the top gates and sluices, ground and gate are all closed.

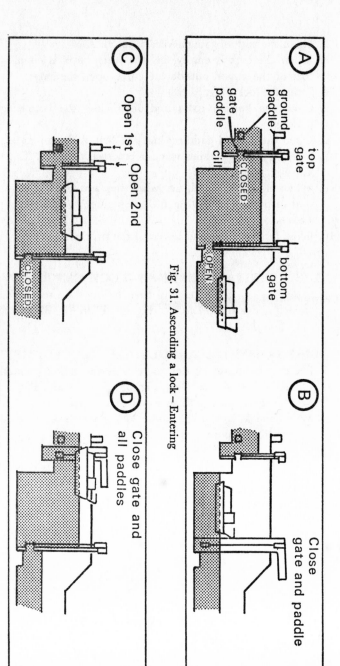

A

top gate

ground paddle

gate paddle

cill

CLOSED

OPEN

bottom gate

Fig. 31. Ascending a lock – Entering

B

Close gate and paddle

C

Open 1st   Open 2nd

CLOSED

Fig. 32. Ascending a lock – Filling and leaving

D

Close gate and all paddles

75

2. Open the bottom gate paddles. (Fig. 31 'A')
3. When the lock is empty, i.e. the water level is equal with that of the pound outside the gates, open the gates.
4. Enter the lock. (Fig. 31 'B')
5. Close the bottom gates and then close the bottom gate paddles.
6. Open the ground paddles slowly at first at the top gates.
7. Open top gate paddles when submerged. (Fig. 32 'C'), (see also Fig. 35)
8. When the lock is full, i.e. when the lock level is equal to that of the top pound, open the top gates. (Fig. 32 'D')
9. Leave the lock.
10. Close the top gates and lower all the paddles.

GOING UPHILL (ASCENDING) – LOCK EMPTY

1. Open the bottom gates and then follow the procedure described above from 4 to 10. (Fig. 31 'B' to Fig. 32 'D')

GOING DOWNHILL (DESCENDING) – LOCK EMPTY

1. See that the bottom gates and sluices are properly closed.
2. Open the ground paddles. (Fig. 33 'E'), (see also Fig. 35)
3. Open the top gate paddles when submerged.
4. When the lock is full, i.e. the lock water level is equal to that of the top pound, open the top gates.
5. Enter the lock. (Fig. 33 'F').
6. Close the top gates and then close the gate paddles and ground paddles.
7. Open the bottom gate paddles, having warned any craft below the lock that you are about to do so. (Fig. 34 'G')
8. When the lock has emptied to the lower level, open the bottom gates.
9. Leave the lock. (Fig. 34 'H')
10. Close the bottom gates and lower the paddles.

GOING DOWNHILL (DESCENDING) – LOCK FULL

1. Open the top gates and then follow the procedure described above from 5 to 10. (Fig. 33 'F' to Fig. 34 'H').

It may be that you come across a lock where the ground

76

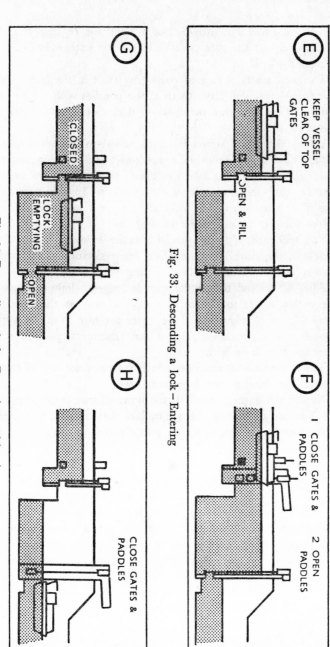

E

KEEP VESSEL
CLEAR OF TOP
GATES

OPEN & FILL

Fig. 33. Descending a lock – Entering

F

1 CLOSE GATES   2 OPEN
PADDLES   PADDLES

G

CLOSED

LOCK
EMPTYING

OPEN

Fig. 34. Descending a lock – Emptying and leaving

H

CLOSE GATES &
PADDLES

sluices are either not provided or are not usable, and you will have to rely on the gate paddles in the top gates only in order to work the lock.

To avoid waterlogging or damaging craft in the lock at the lower level you will have to treat the paddles with the utmost caution. Fig. 36 shows the method that should be adopted in this case.

Whilst the figure shows the rack raised to half-way for the initial fill, it should be raised very slowly, and any sign that the craft is in danger should be dealt with by dropping the paddle slightly until the water level settles down. In this particular case the 'two-thirds full' rule should be rigorously applied, before winding the rack to its topmost limit.

You will probably note that it is easier to swing a gate if its paddle is up, since the gate offers less resistance to the water in this condition. Also, when dealing with a top gate, if the paddles are closed before the gate is opened, slight leakage at the bottom gates may drop the level slightly so that the top gates are effectively jammed by water pressure from the upper pound. Therefore, always leave the closure of paddles until after the gates have been swung.

There are various practices which you may see on the canals which are to be deplored. Here are a few :

Nosing the gates open with the bow of your craft. Don't do it! You may damage the gates, but they are usually pretty rugged so that it is more likely that you will damage your own craft.

Opening the top gate paddles of an empty lock so that the water pressure slams the bottom gates shut. Don't do it! The bottom gates may slam so hard that they are damaged and you may in consequence never fill the lock. The same rule applies to opening the bottom gate paddles of a full lock to slam the top gates shut. It is supposed to be time-saving. It may be for some but for others it probably means hours of repair work and possible closure of the lock.

Closing paddles by releasing the pawl on the ratchet and letting the rack fall under the weight of the paddle. It sometimes may shut off the sluice more effectively but the shock can shear the paddle gear and then no one will be able to use the gear until it is repaired.

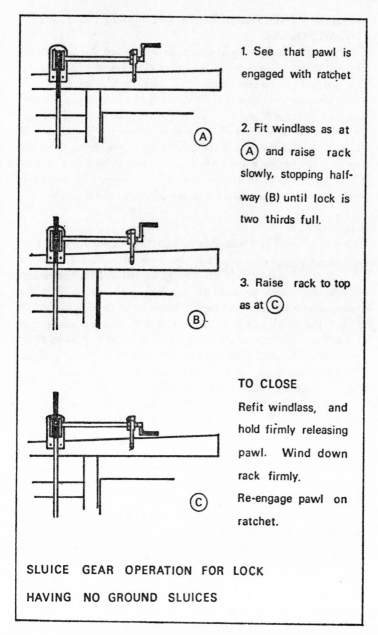

1. See that pawl is engaged with ratchet

2. Fit windlass as at (A) and raise rack slowly, stopping halfway (B) until lock is two thirds full.

3. Raise rack to top as at (C)

TO CLOSE

Refit windlass, and hold firmly releasing pawl. Wind down rack firmly.
Re-engage pawl on ratchet.

SLUICE GEAR OPERATION FOR LOCK
HAVING NO GROUND SLUICES

Fig. 36. Top gate lock drill (No ground sluices)

ALWAYS WIND PADDLES DOWN CAREFULLY WITH THE WINDLASS

On leaving a lock, unless otherwise instructed by the waterway authority, always leave the gates closed and paddles shut. This helps to conserve water. The Thames Conservancy, you will have noted, request that locks should be left empty but this is not an invariable rule for other waterways. In the Fens you are requested to leave lock gates and sluices in the position in which you find them when approaching the lock, as the river flow in many cases is controlled by the sluices and this in turn has to be watched in connection with drainage and irrigation points which are the serious concern of the Fenland farmers.

SIDE-PONDS

Water to a canal is a valuable commodity, especially as it may have to be pumped or piped to the topmost level, for, unlike a river, a canal cannot rely on springs or natural reservoirs and various tributaries to keep it supplied with water. For this reason, side-ponds are provided at some locks to conserve water, so that the total water contents of a lock are not discharged to the lower pound every time the lock is worked. Always make use of the side-pond if one is provided and is in working order. The side-pond is, in fact, a closed chamber at the side of the lock, connected to it by a ground sluice or culvert.

When entering a full lock which has a side-pond, draw the side-pond sluice first. The control gear is similar to that of the ground paddle and is usually set about half-way down the lock-side. The water level, in the lock will fall, ideally to about half-way between the two working levels, unless a previous user has filled it and it has not been emptied again, in which case the level will only drop by about a quarter. Close the side-pond paddle and then proceed to lock out in the normal manner. (Fig. 37, 1, 2 & 3.)

From the lower level, enter the lock and close the bottom gates and sluices and then draw the side-pond sluice. The level should rise to somewhere between a quarter and a half at which point the side-pond paddle is closed and the top gate ground and gate paddles can be opened to continue the locking process.

ALWAYS CLOSE THE SIDE-POND PADDLES BEFORE USING THE TOP OR BOTTOM GATE PADDLES,

OTHERWISE THE PURPOSE OF THE SIDE-POND WILL
BE DESTROYED.

In some cases, it should be noted that paired locks, i.e. those
constructed side by side can be used as side-ponds for each
other, as an interconnecting sluiceway is provided between the
two. Boats can therefore pass one another, one using each lock.
The boat at the upper level enters a full lock, the boat at the
lower level entering the other, empty lock. Gates and paddles
are shut. The interconnecting paddle is drawn so that one
boat falls and the other rises to half level. The centre paddle is
closed and locking continues as normal, the ascending crew
opening the top-gate paddles and the descending crew opening
the bottom gate paddles of their respective locks. Such locks
are to be found on the Grand Union Canal.

Bargemen in a hurry often are observed to ignore the side-
ponds due to the fractionally longer time it takes to lock through
by this method. If the side-pond is in good order, though, it is
no excuse to follow suit. As already explained, time is money
to these people.

LOCK FLIGHTS AND STAIRCASES

In hilly country it is often necessary to arrange sets of locks
close to one another since there is a maximum to which any
lock can be worked in water level, due to the weight of water
involved, bearing in mind the type of lock and gate construction
employed. Modern canals can, of course, nowadays be provided
with very deep locks such as those to be found on the lower
Rhone in Southern France. This has been possible through the
advent of reinforced concrete, electricity (for winding and remote control) and steel. Most canals in the United Kingdom,
however, were constructed before such advances in civil
engineering had been made.

The term 'a flight of locks' refers to a number of separate
locks with very short pounds in between, all rising or falling in
the same direction. Care must be exercised in the use of a flight,
especially having due regard to water conservation and the
avoidance of swamping a lock or pound lower in the line when
making a descent. In most cases a feeder stream runs beside
the flight with small weirs or spillways, to take the excess flow
which may run into the pound, and also to top up a depleted

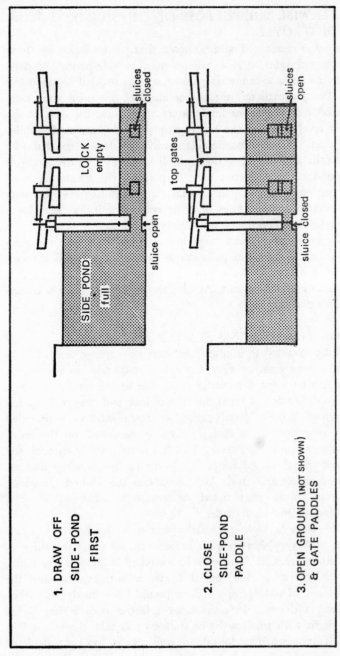

Fig. 37. Paired lock or side-pond working

pound which has been used to discharge into the next lock down. This is also a fairly common practice in France.

On the flight at Bratch, near Birmingham on the Staffordshire and Worcestershire Canal, spillways are provided which take the excess water by a side culvert down to the lowest pound beyond the last lock at the bottom of the flight. This is because the interconnecting pounds are shorter than the locks themselves and are therefore incapable of taking a full lockage of water from the lock above.

If a craft is ascending the flight at the same time as you wish to descend, it is only common sense to wait, unless a proper passing place is provided in one of the intervening pounds between the locks. If neither craft has commenced working through the flight it is better on a short flight to approach the master of the other craft to arrange who is to work the flight first. Remember that if the other vessel is a trading boat then you will be expected to give way in any case.

The lock-working procedure is exactly the same as previously described, each lock being treated as a separate lock. Mention has been made of the flight at Bratch because there are certain precautions which you must take if locking down through full locks. These are explained in the British Waterways Board booklet No. 4 'Cruising on the Staffordshire and Worcestershire Canal'. The essential point is that the spillway inlet should never be covered by an open gate when emptying into the interconnecting pound from a higher lock. Since the inlet is thus blocked off the pound will flood.

Staircase locks are rather more complicated to look at, but under most circumstances are not difficult to work. Full instructions are given in the B.W.B. Cruising Guides as to how they should be worked, and Fig. 38 has been worked out for a particular case to show the principles. This shows the method applicable to three-tier working on any of the three-tier staircases on the Leeds and Liverpool Canal.

The longest staircase in this country at present in operation is on this same canal at Bingley and consists of five interconnecting locks. The method of working this 'five-rise' is exactly similar to that shown for the three-rise shown in the figure. The lock-drill given below is that based on the British Waterways Board instructions which are contained in Inland

Cruising Booklet No. 16, 'Cruising on the Leeds and Liverpool Canal', published by the Board.

Working a staircase is not complicated if you wish to ascend and all the locks are full. In principle you merely have to empty the bottom lock (C), open the gates, enter the lock and close the gates and sluices behind you and open the ground sluices and gate sluices in front of you which will fill your lock, (C) and empty lock (B) to a uniform level so that you can enter lock (B). The procedure is repeated to reach lock (A) and again to reach the top pound.

In the opposite direction, if all the locks are empty or, ideally if (B) and (C) are empty, (A) being full, the lockage of water in (A) is taken through the staircase with you. From (A), you fill (B) to empty (A) which means you can open the gates into (B) and proceed. Close the bottom gates of (A) which are the top gates of (B) behind you and close the sluices and then fill (C) from (B). Proceed into (C) when the levels in (B) and (C) are equal and then empty (C) into the pound below so that you clear (C).

In all cases, when you have used the staircases you are asked, on this particular canal to open one gate paddle leading into (A) so that this lock is always full, an advantage to craft travelling in either direction.

The complicated part arises where you arrive at the top of the staircase and find all the locks full, or where you arrive at the bottom and find all the locks empty. In the former case, the normal drill will cause the water in (A) to swamp lock (B) and flood over the top of the gates into (C) and so on, a practice which is to be discouraged at all costs. In the latter, you will have insufficient water to float your craft and without water to float you up to the top gates of (C) to enable you to open them into (B), etc.

The figure shows the arrangement of locks and the working of them for descending with all locks full at the start (Fig. 38 – Diag. I).

GOING DOWNHILL (DESCENDING) – LOCKS FULL

1. Open top gates of lock (A) and enter.
2. Close top gates of lock (A) and ensure that the ground and gate paddles are also closed.

3. Walk down to lock (C) and half-open the ground paddles.
4. Walk back to lock (B) and half-open the ground paddles.
5. Return to Lock (A) and open both ground and gate paddles slowly, taking care not to allow lock (B) to flood.

} Fig. 38
Diag. II

6. When the water in lock (A) has fallen to the level of that in lock (B), close the ground paddle in lock (B), leading to (C).
7. Open the top gates of lock (B) and proceed into the lock. (Fig. 38, III)
8. Close the top gates and ground paddle (A-B) and the top gate sluices of lock (B).
9. Return to lock (A) and open ONE gate paddle.
10. Open the ground and gate paddles at the top gate of lock (C) slowly taking care not to allow lock (C) to flood.
11. When the water in lock (B) has fallen to the level of lock (C) close the ground paddles at the bottom gates of lock (C).
12. Open the top gates of lock (C) and enter the lock.
13. Close the gates and the attendant ground and gate paddles.
14. Open the ground and gate paddles fully at the bottom of lock (C) having warned craft who may be waiting below. (Fig. 38, IV)
15. When the water level in lock (C) has fallen to that of the pound below, open the bottom gates of lock (C) and leave the lock.
16. Close the gates at the bottom of lock (C) and the ground and gate paddles.

The craft waiting below have now to deal with a staircase of empty locks which they wish to ascend. This is the other awkward case we mentioned.

GOING UPHILL (ASCENDING) – LOCKS EMPTY
1. Open gates at bottom of lock (C) and enter lock.
2. Close ground and gate paddles, or see that they are closed, at bottom gates of lock (C).
3. Walk up to locks (B) and (A) and half open the ground paddles.

4. Proceed to the top gate of lock (A) and half open the ground paddle beside the top pound, to fill lock (A).
5. Wait until lock (C) is full and then close ground paddles (A-B) and top pound to (A).
6. Open gates into lock (B) and enter lock.
7. Close ground paddles at bottom of lock (B) and also gate paddles.
8. Open ground and gate paddles at top of lock (B).
9. When lock (B) is full open top gates and enter lock (A).
10. Close bottom gates of lock (A) and ground and gate paddles.
11. Open ground and gate paddles at top of lock (A).
12. When lock (A) is full open gates and leave lock.
13. Close top gates of lock (A) and close ground and gate paddles.

Two-tier staircases generally dispense with the need to half-open ground paddles in order to fill the lock above the lower one, when ascending or to empty the lower lock if descending. It is usually better to start, when ascending, by filling the top lock in the normal manner, closing the top lock, top gate and ground paddles and then transferring the lockage of water to the lower lock by means of the central gate and ground paddles. The central gates can then be opened and the top lock dealt with as though it was a single lock as in Fig. 31 (B) and 32 (C & D).

If descending with full locks, empty the bottom lock out first and then lock through in the normal manner, treating the two-tier locks as (B) and (C) in Fig. 38 and following the drill from 10 to 16, above.

STAIRCASE VARIATIONS

You will probably find variations to the construction of staircase locks, since different engineers were responsible for their design. On the narrow canals it is quite common to find that the interconnecting gates possess no gate paddles, so that you are obliged to use the ground paddles only. Such staircases are to be found at Grindley Brook on the Llangollen Canal and the Northgate flight at Chester on the Shropshire Union, although the latter is not strictly a narrow canal at this point, being 13 feet 2 inches wide. Full instructions as to their use is given in the British Waterways Board cruising booklets which are essential. Com-

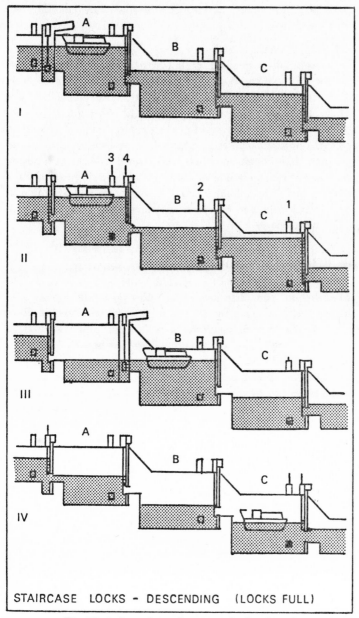

STAIRCASE LOCKS - DESCENDING (LOCKS FULL)

Fig. 38. A three-tier staircase on the Leeds and
Liverpool Canal

pared with the mine of information that they contain their price is nominal.

FRENCH STAIRCASES

There is another method of staircase working which is not used in this country, but which may be of interest, particularly to anyone thinking of trying their hand on the French canals. Where locks are in good condition and plentiful supply of water is available at the head of the canal the following method is used, possibly because it reduces locking time. It should also be noted that French locks are all manned by keepers who are well versed in the method of operation. If you do have to use a staircase and this method worked, pay very careful attention to their instructions and be ready to move your craft as soon as instructed to do so.

GOING UPHILL (ASCENDING) – LOCKS EMPTY

All lock gates except the top gates of the staircase will be OPEN. Enter the bottom lock. The gates and paddles will be closed behind you. The keeper will now go to the top gates of the top lock and open the sluices. The water will cascade down over the cills of each successive lock (a most impressive and, to some, terrifying sight) eventually filling the bottom lock to its top level. At this point your vessel must move into the next lock. The gates are closed behind you as well as the paddles and you continue to rise to the top level of this lock. When cleared by the keeper, move forward again. The process is repeated until you are finally at the top when the top lock fills to enable the top gates to be open and you can leave the lock.

The process for descending when the locks are full is similar to the English system but instead of opening the ground paddles half-way in the lower locks the keeper will probably empty each lock in turn at full bore successively up the chain. As you lock through each lock, however the back gates will probably be left open if no further traffic is expected as you descend.

French lock-keepers on little used stretches of canal have a telephone system between locks. Always let them know if you are stopping for lunch or are thinking of turning round to retrace your route. This will save them time and trouble as you will often find your progress being reported along the length of the canal and a delay may cause them worry, and a turn-round will probably mean that a lock-keeper has made his lock ready for you for nothing. This does not apply on the commercial waterways, of course, but here a tip of about 1 franc is always appreciated. On smaller canals, the tip is not expected. A cigarette, however is often appreciated for any extra service that these friendly people may give you.

LOCK TROUBLES AND SIMPLE CURES

Occasionally one comes across trouble in working a lock. Major difficulties arising from broken gear, such as paddles etc. must be referred to the waterway authority immediately, if you can reach a telephone, if no official is about. As stated before, if the gates are padlocked you must on no account use the lock, unless you have been given the keys, as in the case of the River Nene. If you had planned your route carefully and consulted the authority, however, this state of affairs should not arise as you will have been forewarned of the closure.

One particular occurrence that is a nuisance is that the gates become jammed. Check first that your water levels are correct so that the gates should open, and if levels are definitely correct, the first procedure is to post a crew member or more than one on each balance beam and get them to 'waggle' the balance beams applying pressure simultaneously to each gate. If this does not do the trick, you may find that some gates can be prised apart by a hefty balk of wood inserted through the iron stanchions which may run along the cat-walk of the gates where one is provided.

It may be, of course that the gates are jammed below the water line by rubbish or a waterlogged tree stump which has floated down on the current. At some locks, you will find an extra long boat-hook or tree-hook (often lying half-hidden in the grass) which may assist you to clear the obstruction by dragging the base of the gates on the top side. Obstructions can also lodge in the crevice between the lock wall and the heel post. Use the hook to clear these out and try the gates again. As a last resort you might try bringing the bow of your craft up to the mitre of the gates very gently and then engaging forward gear and opening the throttle, but note that this practice is strongly discouraged and any damage you do will attract heavy penalties.

The other snag that may be encountered is where the gates refuse to shut properly. This again is usually caused by debris in the heel-post crevice which should be cleared, or foreign matter getting trapped between the gate and its cill. In the latter case, open the gates and run the hook along the back of the cill to clear the obstruction and try closing the gates again. If they are not a tight fit, opening the top gate sluices will probably seal them by virtue of the water pressure brought into the lock, if the trouble is at the bottom gates. If the trouble occurs at the top gates, lowering the water level in the lock by opening the bottom gate sluices should do the trick.

Faulty sluice-gear can be got round in an emergency. If jammed shut there is little or no problem if only one sluice is jammed. It will just take you a little longer to lock through, using the others. If jammed open, it will be possible to use the lock but a considerable amount of water will pass through the lock and it will take you a lot longer to fill or empty the lock as the case may be.

ON NO ACCOUNT INTERFERE WITH BROKEN SLUICE GEAR.

GUILLOTINE GATES

On some rivers and in one or two isolated cases on the canals, but mainly on the Fenland network from Bedford to King's Lynn the locks are provided at one end with a guillotine gate. This is a single flat steel gate which rises and falls in guides in the lock-sides and is operated by geared winches to an over-head pulley on a gantry.

No separate sluice is provided in the gate. To empty or fill the lock as the case may be, the gate is 'broken' by raising it six inches. As soon as the levels are equated the gate is raised to its full extent to allow craft to pass beneath. In one or two cases the gate is raised and then pivots, to swing into a horizontal position to give even greater head-room. A few are electrically operated by lock-keepers, a few hand-operated by the keepers and others have to be worked by boat crews. The opposite end of the lock can have the double 'mitred' gates or a single 'clapper' gate which spans the river at right-angles.

In isolated cases the guillotine may form the top and not the bottom gate of the lock, which is the more usual position.

GUARD LOCKS

Guard locks are located at the downstream end of a river section of canal where it has made use of that part of the river for its course. In average weather conditions guard locks are left open, so that craft may proceed unhindered. In times of flood, however they are brought into use to prevent the river flooding the canal section beyond and are worked in the normal way.

Guard locks are also sometimes found at canal junctions, entries to docks etc., but they should not be confused with tidal locks, such as the one at Richmond on the Thames or those that exist at dock entries in estuaries or harbours.

SUMMARY

1. The best way to get through locks is to follow the 'lock drill' through systematically. Those not familiar with this should study the relevant paragraphs of the lock-working section.

2. Note that damage can result from forcing gates open by craft.

3. While in a lock chamber a craft should be secured where possible and attended to allow for movement up or down as the water level changes. Craft must not be made fast to lock-gate fixtures, paddle posts, or other fittings. Bollards should be used where provided. Craft must be kept clear of lock cills.

4. To conserve water, gate and ground paddles must be securely and fully closed on leaving the lock.

5. Powered locks must only be operated by the waterway authority's staff. Such locks may be manually operated if absolutely necessary and subject to the authority's permission.

6. Locks which are shut with chains or by other methods must not be interfered with unless the authority has provided you with the necessary keys.

7. Details of lock availability times should always be checked with the local office of the waterway authority concerned. These times vary and are not normally advertised in the bye-laws.

SECTION V

MOVABLE BRIDGES, ETC.

General
Lift Bridges
Swing Bridges
Unmanned Bridges
Bridge Drill
Aqueducts

SECTION V

MOVABLE BRIDGES ETC.

GENERAL

In many places where the building of canals interfered with farm lands by cutting through territory in one ownership on either side of the canal, the canal builders were obliged to give the farmer access across the canal. In odd cases this was done by means of a ferry, more commonly by means of a brick-built bridge and yet in others, possibly through cost or technical reasons, by means of a swing or lift bridge. Canal engineering also called for other features, such as aqueducts, lifts, inclined planes and tunnels, the latter already having been discussed in Section I.

LIFT BRIDGES

Lift bridges fall into two main categories; (a) those that are counterbalanced and (b) those that are *not* counterbalanced. The former are more common.

Fig. 39 shows a typical example of a counterbalanced lift bridge as found on the southern section of the Oxford Canal. To raise the bridge, the operator merely pulls down the balance beam by means of the chain and the bridge section swings upwards out of the way of the vessel passing on the canal. If negotiating such a bridge, the helmsman should steer well clear of the pivoted side of the bridge as obviously his headroom increases to the left as shown in the figure.

The bridge is pivoted on a quadrant which turns on metal teeth set on the ground as shown in the second illustration. You should be warned that this type of bridge can be very unstable in a high wind blowing across the canal. Never send children to operate the bridge on their own. With the wind blowing from right to left in the figure, the raised road section acts as a considerable wind-brake and can easily come crashing down as there is often no fixing point for the balance beam when it is in the lowered (bridge up) position. It is therefore advisable for the 'bridgeman' to lend his weight to the beam by sitting on it until you have cleared the bridge.

The other type of counterbalance bridge is that found on the Llangollen Canal which has additional overhead beams and is reminiscent of bridges shown in the paintings of the old Flemish masters. The method of operation, however, is similar to that described above, although the transfer of weight in the overhead beam ensures that they are not as sensitive to the wind. Some lifting bridges of this type are worked by electric winch, but in these cases they are manned by bridge-keepers. All that is required of the navigator is one long blast on the horn or whistle if necessary.

Some lift bridges, particularly those on the continent, are not counter balanced, but are winched by electricity or gear and windlass, being supported in the up position by the winding cable. The drive shafts of the manual type are usually fitted with a dog of the same dimensions as the lock paddle gear, so that the boat windlass will fit them.

SWING BRIDGES

The alternative type of movable bridge is the swing bridge. This consists of a swinging platform which is balanced on a central turning pivot or trunnion which is usually mounted to one side of the canal. Only one side of the total moving bridge section

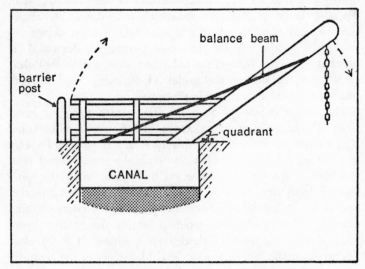

Fig. 39. Simple counter-balanced lift bridge

therefore actually traverses the canal. The methods of operation fall into two main categories for those operated by the boatman. Either the bridge is balanced to be easily moved by hand or a gear mechanism is provided which can be turned by fitting the lock windlass to a shaft beside the bridge on one or other bank. Operation, merely consists of raising a catch and pushing the bridge round or winding it round.

Manned swing bridges exist where major roads cross a canal or on busy commercial waterways. If necessary at these you may sound one long blast on your horn to advise the bridge-man of your approach. Never assume that a manned bridge will open immediately. Traffic conditions on the carriageway may not permit it. NEVER try and shoot a swing or lift bridge if you have any doubts as to its headroom or the maximum height of your own craft above the waterline.

On the Norfolk Broads, where railway swing bridges still exist they are only opened for coastal craft and sea-going pleasure craft which cannot lower their canopies or masts. If you have hired a motor cruiser from a Broads yard, ALWAYS lower your canopy where advised by notice-board on the bridge itself or by the owners or their agents. Broads sailing hire-craft are constructed to be able to lower their masts quickly as there

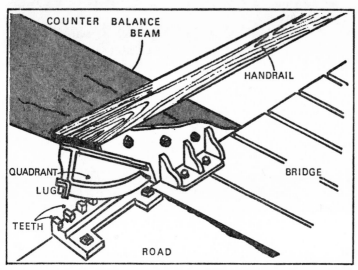

Fig. 40. Lift bridge pivot details

is an agreement that the railway authority will not swing the bridges for these craft.

On the Broads and many other wide waterways the central pier on which the bridge swings may be in the centre of the waterway. Always check on the chart as to which side of the pier you must pass. Look out for notices and bridge marks, if any, at such places. In the absence of any indication you may safely assume that you should keep to the rule of the river which dictates that you leave a central pier to PORT, i.e. you pass to the right of it.

UNMANNED BRIDGES (LIFT AND SWING)
BRIDGE DRILL

On approaching a lift or swing bridge, moor to the bank most convenient for your purpose, (usually on the towpath side) so that one or more members of your crew can go ahead to open the bridge. Wait well clear of the bridge until it is properly raised and they have signalled that you may proceed.

The bridge party should follow the drill given below :
1. Check that no traffic is within a reasonable distance of the bridge.
2. Cross to the opposite side of the bridge from where it is pivoted and raise or fasten across the roadway the barrier provided.
3. Raise the bridge and secure it if possible, or swing the bridge and drop the securing catch, if provided.
4. Signal the helmsman that he has clear passage, if no other craft is coming in the opposite direction.
5. When your craft is through, lower or swing back the bridge and secure, if possible.
6. Remove the road barrier.

NOTE

You should not leave the bridge in the 'open' position for other craft unless such is within 200 yards of the bridge and has signified (by one long blast on its horn) that it wishes to use the bridge. Those operated by windlass should be treated with extreme caution, as careless handling can cause the windlass to fly back. Moor up your craft, again to the towpath, just sufficiently long to retrieve your bridge party and then proceed.

As in the case of locks, NEVER moor close to a movable bridge as you will hinder other craft who wish to use it.

AQUEDUCTS
An aqueduct, as its name implies, carries water across lower terrain by means of a bridge, rather than by an embankment. There are still a number of fine examples in this country, two on the Llangollen Canal at Pontcysyllte across the River Dee, being 1,007 feet long and at Chirk across the River Ceriog being 710 feet long. A unique structure is the Barton Swing Aqueduct on the Bridgewater Canal, which was built in 1893. Holding 1,500 tons of water the aqueduct can be swung, full, in order to allow passage to ocean-going ships on the Manchester Ship Canal below it. This aqueduct is manned and operated by electricity.

Navigate aqueducts with extreme caution and lower your speed. Keep children where you can see them and do not enter an aqueduct section if craft are coming towards you as the section is often necessarily narrow, and you will not be able to pass mid-way across.

SECTION VI

KNOTS AND ROPEWORK

Knots
Splices
Whippings
Rope Handling

Illustrations

SECTION VI

KNOTS AND ROPEWORK

KNOTS

The over-rated reef-knot is shown in the accompanying illustrations. It is used for reefing and also for tying parcels. If you want to use it anywhere else there is probably a better knot for the job, although it CAN be used for joining two ropes of equal thickness and is also used in whippings which are explained later. Remember the rule : 'Right over left – left over right.'

For joining wet ropes together the fisherman's knot is to be preferred. This is formed by tying two overhand knots, one on each line round the standing part of the other and pulling the two together. To undo, merely pull the knots apart by taking hold of the free ends and opening the knots up. Even though the ropes are wet it should now be fairly easy to undo the overhand knots.

The figure of eight knot is useful, especially to stop a rope slipping through a fairlead or bullseye which would be found as a fender fastening or sheet end stopper.

The sheet bend is the knot for joining ropes of differing thickness. Do NOT use a reef knot for this purpose. It *will* slip. The sheet bend can also be used for ropes of equal thickness and is, perhaps, a quicker knot to make.

The Bowline. One of the most important knots for mooring purposes. The basis is a knot which will leave a loop permanently formed which will not vary in size. It can be used for dropping over a bollard or pile cap, and has the advantage over a hitch that the knot itself can be undone away from the bollard if a large enough loop is formed. A running Bowline is formed by passing the standing part of the rope back through the loop and forming a second one. This is far safer than the common slip knot formed by an overhand knot at the end of a loop. There is a rule for remembering how to tie the bowline : 'Make a hole and pass the rabbit up through the hole, round the back of the tree and down the hole again.' Pull up tight. Childish perhaps? But an effective memory aid.

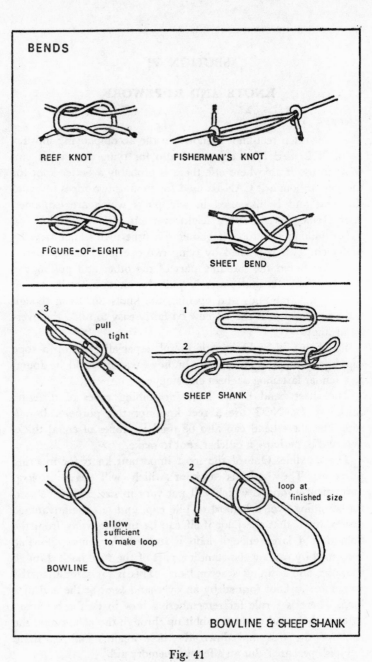

Fig. 41

HITCHES

The Mooring Hitch is useful if lines have been brought ashore and are found to be too long. Form a loop and, taking the loop round the mooring post, pass its head under itself and draw up tight. Now take the free end and pass it through the loop and draw this up tight. If the line is still too long, make the free end into another loop before passing it through the first. To undo, merely pull the free end, take the strain off the standing part and either lift or pull the knot off the post.

The Clove Hitch is useful for mooring and also for securing a rope to a spar where it is essential there will be no sideways movement when under strain. It can be formed by making two loops in any part of the rope and dropped over a post as shown in the illustration. Alternatively it can be threaded round a post or spar as shown.

The Rolling hitch is a useful knot as it will not slip when executed round a sail spar, hanging off a rope on a stopper or for a flag swivel stick. It is not ideal for mooring purposes however, but will remain firm against lateral strain.

The Round Turn and Two Half Hitches is self-explanatory in its title. It can be used for mooring as shown or for fastening a warp to a ring or handle.

The fisherman's bend is a more sophisticated version of the previous knot being more secure. It is therefore more advisable to use this knot especially for where fastening to anchor rings etc. where undoing of the knot accidentally would be disastrous. As an added precaution the free end is often tied to the standing part with twine after the knot has been secured.

Fig. 41 shows the much joked about Sheep Shank. It is used for shortening a rope which will be under permanent strain. Take care when this is used, as if the strain is taken off the rope the loops may fall out of the hitches and the knot's purpose be destroyed.

On Fig. 43 is shown the Tug Boat Hitch. This is a useful quick hitch when mooring up temporarily as might happen if you are working a lock single handed or taking on a passenger at a jetty. Take two turns up the bollard and then make a loop under the turns passing it over the top of the bollard. Further loops can be made as shown in the second illustration.

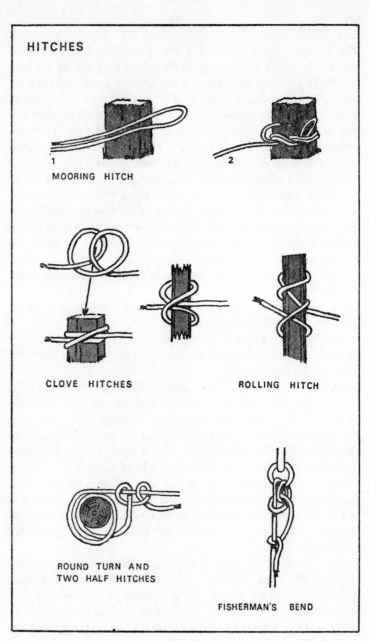

HITCHES

1 MOORING HITCH 2

CLOVE HITCHES

ROLLING HITCH

**ROUND TURN AND
TWO HALF HITCHES**

FISHERMAN'S BEND

Fig. 42

CLEATS

It is surprising how many text books ignore the correct way to fasten a rope to a cleat. Three methods are shown here in Fig. 44 and 45.

The first is where a quick release is required and should not be left permanently on the cleat. This is known as the Slippery Hitch in which an 'S' is made round the cleat and a loop formed and passed under the part of the rope that lies across the top of the cleat. To release, merely pull the end and unwind. Always take a turn round the base of the cleat first.

For a more secure hitch to a cleat make two figures of eight, having first started with a turn round the cleat. Then make a loop with the free end tucked under the standing part and pass it over the jaw of the cleat towards the strain. Always start with the first turn on the post of the cleat furthest from the strain. Note that excessive figures of eight are to be deplored. Two are the maximum sufficient in any case. Some seamen point out that the hitch over the jaw of the cleat is prone to tighten, especially if the rope is under continual strain or becomes wet. The alternative is to make two figures of eight and then wind the rope round the base of the cleat until the free end can be pulled tight to jam under the turns above it. No knot or hitch is made so that to undo, the end is pulled free and unwound.

CROWN KNOT

If you have not the twine or time to stop the end of a rope from fraying, a quick method is to tie a crown knot with the strands as follows :

Unlay the rope for six to seven times its diameter in length and splay out the ends, holding them upright. Ignore the rear strand of the three to start with and pass the left hand strand to the right over the right hand strand which in turn is passed under the top strand. Make a bigger loop with the top-most strand by passing it back again to the left. Now take the rear strand, curling it forward over the top strand where it has run back to the left and under the upper part of the small loop of the middle strand. Pull it down and then tighten and trim all three ends.

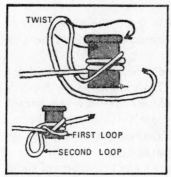

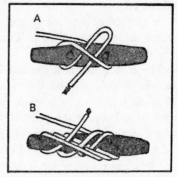

Fig. 43. The Tug Boat Hitch

Fig. 44. 'Slippery Hitch' (A) and Permanent Hitch (B)

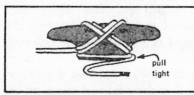

Fig. 45. 'Jammed' turn

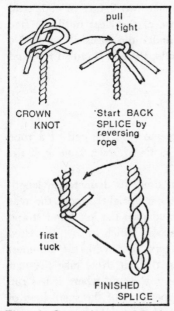

Fig. 46. Crown knot and back splice

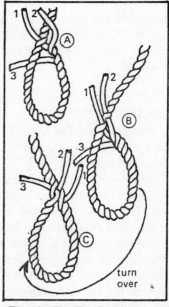

Fig. 47. The Eye-Splice

SPLICING

We now come to the splicing of ropes, the commonest you will require being the back splice and the eye-splice, very useful for fender fastenings. The eye-splice is used to attach the fender to its rope and the back splice is worked on the other end of the fender rope to stop the end fraying out. In many cases the back splice is sturdier than a whipping, but has the disadvantage that it doubles the thickness of the rope at the end. Whippings are therefore dealt with in the next part of this section.

THE BACK SPLICE

Start the back splice by unlaying the rope eight to nine times its diameter and tying a crown knot with the strands (see diagram in Fig. 46 and description above). Hold the rope's end towards you and take one strand and pass it over the next strand of the standing part of the rope to the left and under the next. Pull the end through. Taking the next strand to the left, repeat the same procedure, and repeat again with the third strand. You should now have each strand projecting from a separate part of the lay. Take the first strand again and pass it over the left hand strand of the standing part, tuck under the next strand of the standing part and pull through. Repeat to make a second round of tucks with the remaining ends, making sure that the over and under rule is applied only to strands of the standing part of the rope. Do NOT confuse these with the ends coming back up the rope. Always work round the rope, taking ends from right to left, turning the rope clockwise.

Keep pulling the ends up tight and after the third round of tucks, trim the ends off, not too close or they will pull out. Place the spliced end on the ground and roll it under the foot to take out any unevenness.

THE EYE-SPLICE

Fig. 47 shows how to start off the eye-splice. Take the standing part of the rope and, holding the end towards you, unlay the rope for eight or nine diameters in length. Take the unlaid ends round to the right and pass the first and second strands over the top of the standing part, leaving the third below it. Tuck the first and second strands under the lay as shown, one above the other and pull through, tightly, ignoring the third strand. Now turn the loop over as shown at position 'C', take the third strand and pass it through the next lay up the rope from right to left. Continue with a second and third round of tucks as described for the back splice.

THE SHORT SPLICE

This is useful for joining two ropes together more permanently than by knotting. A splice does not weaken the breaking strain of a rope as much as a knot, but it should be pointed out that the long splice which is more difficult to execute is more reliable. Knowledge of this latter splice is not required within the syllabus of the R.Y.A. Certificates so is not shown but details may be found in Reed's Almanac. Again, with the short splice it is advisable to complete the splice with three rounds of tucks in each direction. Having completed the three rounds on the left hand side of the figure above, unseize the temporary stopping and complete the splice to the right.

WHIPPINGS

The only whipping worth doing is the one that does not come undone and this is known as the 'Sailmaker's Whipping'. First of all we must explain the laying of a rope. Most ropes are composed of three strands, wound in an anti-clockwise direction. The strands themselves are composed of fibres which are wound in a clockwise direction so that the fibres lie parallel to the direction of the strain. When relaying a rope by twisting the strands together, each strand should therefore be twisted between thumb and forefinger in the opposite direction to which the strand is being laid. These factors are most important to remember when whipping the end of a rope and also coiling down, with which we shall also deal in the next heading of this section.

Whipping prevents a rope end fraying. Modern ropes of nylon and other synthetics can be protected by heat sealing, but as soon as one is cut or broken how successful an amateur heat seal with a match or cigarette lighter can be is questionable. The method is shown in Fig. 49. The correct material to use is sail twine but nylon string is an effective substitute. The twine or string should be wax coated. The writers use the stump of a

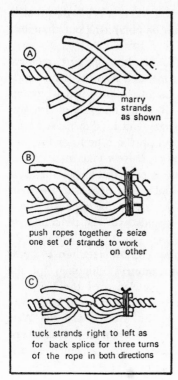

marry strands as shown

push ropes together & seize one set of strands to work on other

tuck strands right to left as for back splice for three turns of the rope in both directions

Fig. 48. The Short Splice

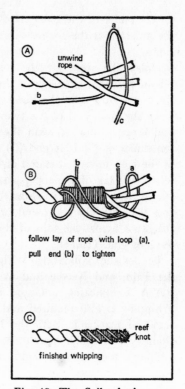

unwind rope

a

b

c

follow lay of rope with loop (a).

pull end (b) to tighten

reef knot

finished whipping

Fig. 49. The Sailmaker's Whipping

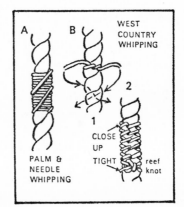

A

B

WEST COUNTRY WHIPPING

2

1

CLOSE UP TIGHT

PALM & NEEDLE WHIPPING

reef knot

Fig. 50. Palm and Needle and West Country Whippings

candle and pass the twine across it, making a fairly deep cut in the grease, but the proper wax can be obtained from chandlery stores.

Unlay the rope for the length of the whipping required (about twice the diameter of the rope) and pass the twine inside the centre strand at the lower point of the proposed whipping. Take the short end of the twine (B) down one side of the rope and form a loop (A) with the longer end as shown. With the remainder of the long end (C) wind up the rope from the start of the loop towards the end of the rope. Now take the loop and follow the lay of the rope, passing it over the top of the same strand from which it was started and pull it tight with the short end (B). Pass the short end up the lay of the rope and tie a reef knot across the tops of the strands with the remainder of the long end. Trim off.

Besides the Sailmakers' Whipping you are required to know the Palm and Needle and West Country Whippings for the R.Y.A. Certificates in Grade II. Knowledge of the Common Whipping is also required and this may be referred to in any standard text-book. Both the Palm and Needle and the West Country are much simpler to execute than the Sailmakers' although they appear more complex, being executed in the length of a rope and not necessarily at the end. They are extremely useful as chafe protection where ropes run through blocks or on the bights of eye-splices.

THE PALM AND NEEDLE WHIPPING
Take a length of twine and leaving a fair length at the end start winding it tightly against the lay of the rope for the length required. Thread the trailing end (the end where you started) through the rope so that it passes behind one strand with the needle. Use the palm if you have to but this is not usually necessary. Pull the thread through and leave. Now thread the needle with the other end of twine at the top of the whipping and pass this through the rope, between the strands, so that it protrudes from between two of them but NOT the same two as at the bottom if you follow the lay round. Pass this thread down the outside of the whipping following the lay of the rope and pass it through the rope at the base of the whipping to come out at the third space (i.e. where the trailing end was

inserted). Pass this leading end back up the coil, similarly following the lay and take up the trailing end, following the third depression caused by the lay in the same way. Open the lay at the top by un-twisting the rope and with the aid of the needle, tie a reef knot with the leading and trailing ends across the top of the whipping inside the lay. Trim off the ends.

WEST COUNTRY WHIPPING

This is merely a series of overhand knots made in front of, and behind the rope, started by placing the rope to the centre of the twine. Continue the knots for the length of whipping required, pulling each one tight and finish with a reef knot, trimming the ends.

Common and American Whippings are not shown as the authors do not recommend them. If not executed really tightly they are prone to pulling off the rope if worked on the ends. They are, however suitable for working on the length of a rope but will not stand as much wear as the latter two mentioned above.

ROPE HANDLING

COILING DOWN

There is a correct way to coil a rope so that every time it is picked up it doesn't appear to have knitted itself into a pair of stockings. Remember how a rope is laid, as described under the previous heading. To coil a rope therefore, it is necessary to impart an added twist to the rope as you coil. Hold the standing part of the rope in the left hand and with the right hand lay the running part about three feet away across the palm of the left hand, making a loop from the thumb back round to the little finger in a clockwise direction, at the same time turning the top of the rope with the right hand fingers in towards your left hand, i.e. clockwise as viewed from the free end of the rope.

You can coil in the other direction but it is not as easy, as you may have to let go of the rope with the right hand once in every revolution of coil. Having reached the end, reverse the coil and hang it on the cleat or hook intended with the free end inside or place it neatly on the deck with the free end underneath.

Those neat flat coils that look like catherine wheels are easy to make once you realise that the rope has to be twisted into position as you coil. Start with the free end in the middle and lay out the whole rope, unfastening the standing part temporarily, along the deck. Straighten out any kinks or knots. Turn the free end twisting the rope into the centre of the coil and allow it to build up as it rotates. Walking round it and laying the rope as you go will get you in a frightful muddle and dizzy into the bargain. When complete, refasten the outer end back on to its cleat.

FLAKING DOWN

A rope that has to be paid out quickly is often better flaked down on to the deck in 'criss-cross' fashion. Start from the standing end, running the rope backwards and forwards about four or five times in each direction, so that the lengths lay fairly flat on the deck. Then carry out the same procedure at right angles for the next layer and so on until the end comes out on top. It will then be ready for use, without having to be extricated from the bundle as in the case of the inverted coil.

THROWING A ROPE

The practice of rope throwing between ship and shore is fraught with the most hilarious of possibilities. An advertiser of shaving soap had a catch-phrase, probably borrowed from seafaring men who rarely shaved in the days of sail – 'Not too little ... and not too much.' This maxim applies to rope throwing, in so far as it is important to know just how much of the rope to throw.

Anything thrown through the air relies for its trajectory on weight, shape and windage. (If you're good at ball games – from here on you will have to forget most of what you've learned.) About shape we can do little, except make sure that the coil thrown travels end on rather than sideways. Take the standing part of the rope close to its cleat in the left hand and hold the running part, coiled in the right hand. Judge the distance to be thrown and make sure that when the rope lands it will have two or three turns of the coil left. Any excess in the right hand should be passed in successive loops to the left hand and retained there. The end of the rope will be hanging from the coil closest to the palm of the right hand and will protrude from between thumb and forefinger.

If it does not, the standing part may jerk the coil apart as it unwinds so reverse the coil in the hand. Swing the right arm back and throw forward at shoulder height with the arm outstretched in the manner of a discus thrower, releasing the coil so that it travels horizontally towards the shore. If your instinct tells you that the coil is not going to reach, follow through with the coil from the left hand. For longer throws, it is best to follow this practice anyway. Excess weight in the right hand coil may prevent you getting a good long distance throw in the first place.

Too much coil makes a good throw over short distances but confuses the man on shore, who will probably dance about, looking for the end. Too little and the rope will jerk back into the water and, at worst, it will be devoured by the propeller and the shore party will be immersed in their eagerness to reach it.

Remember to allow for a cross wind by altering the direction of your throw accordingly. With the wind behind you, the job will be simpler, but throwing into a headwind can be tricky. Increased energy may not always be the answer as a strong headwind will easily unravel your coil before it reaches the shore. A thinner or 'heaving' line, led from the main rope can be fastened to a rond anchor or a suitable weight and that thrown, the heavier line being hauled ashore by means of the thinner one when retrieved by the shore party.

There is one important point to remember about being hauled into position from the shore. If the shore party consists of a lot of eager small boys or eager landlubbers unconnected with your crew, make sure that the crew aboard are ready to unship the lines from their cleats! Landlubbers are often known to heave so fast in their enthusiasm that damage will be done to the boat. The only cure is therefore to release your lines and let them heave the whole line ashore rather than strand the craft halfway across a neighbouring ploughed field!

SECTION VII

MOORING

General Principles
Basic Mooring
Floating Moorings – Clearing
Floating Moorings – Picking Up
Winding Ship

Illustrations

SECTION VII

MOORING

GENERAL PRINCIPLES
The choice of location of a good mooring is usually based on experience, local knowledge and common sense, but in order of importance we would venture to suggest that these points should be reversed. It is surprising how little of the latter appears to be evident on the inland waterways these days. Fanatics, new to the motor cruising game need really have no worries, though, since common sense, based on a few essential principles which will be explained here, is the major factor in determining what may and what may not prove a good mooring.

Local knowledge has found its way into most good cruising guides and maps, without which no craft should ever be, if straying further than 100 yards from the boat-yard. Stanford's of London publish excellent maps of the Broads and Thames and have added further with the Fenland Waterways. British Waterways provide booklets of the major canal routes with charts of the canals in strip form. Similar strip maps 'for the Continental waterways published abroad', are available in this country from Captain Watt's and other major chandlers and chart agents.

Lock-keepers are a good source of information on moorings. Their experience and that of other watermen can usually be counted on but beware of advice from the old gent in the peaked cap and the guernsey, wheeling his bike down the tow-path! If his advice conflicts with the common sense solution to your problem, it is better to ignore it. He's probably after mushrooms anyway.

Mooring in prohibited areas is damned bad manners, and also may be illegal. A riparian owner, (the owner of the river bank), has rights of access and under common law, fishing rights and others in connection with irrigation and watering of livestock as far as the centre of the stream, irrespective of whatever navigation rights exist. Navigation rights have, of course, been more and more brought under the control of waterway authorities such as the Thames Conservancy which was founded in 1857 and more latterly the British Waterways Board, the setting up of which effectively nationalised most of the navigable canals and a number of the more important rivers.

These controls, however, only apply to navigation and in some cases water conservation and the banks are still extensively privately owned – even the Thames Conservancy has been forced to purchase land in one or two places for the sole purpose of providing moorings for river users in parts of the Thames where such amenities were not available. Make sure, therefore, that you are not trespassing when mooring your craft.

Suitable moorings are often found against a towpath but here again there is an established code, especially on canals. You will be contravening bye-laws if your mooring ropes cross the path. In many cases you may be guilty of obstructing a right of way, although it is useful to note that a towpath, ipso facto, is not necessarily a right of way. More simply : your ropes stretched across the path are an obvious source of danger. Always drive your mooring irons in on the river or canal side of the path if it is permissible that vessels can moor to the towpath bank at all. In many cases it is not. Where horse or tractor drawn barge traffic is encountered you will find you have no right to moor to the towpath side, since your vessel will foul the tow-ropes of passing craft. In built-up areas especially, make sure that you are not driving your stake through power lines or outfall pipes which may be run across the bed of the river or canal.

Never moor on the inside of a bend, or where the channel or view of the river are restricted. It is unwise to moor immediately below a bridge unless it is one of full span which does not interrupt the helmsman's view of both banks on his approach. Do not moor up in a short lock pound as, in rainy weather, the pound may quickly flood or, alternatively, the lock gates to the lower level may be ill-fitting and the water level might drop appreciably grounding your cruiser overnight. This applies particularly in dry weather and where water is not fed to the pound by a weir stream or siphon.

Bye-laws usually require that mooring should not be permitted within specified distances of locks – anything between

114

100 and 500 yards is quite common, although the latter figure more often applies to waterways carrying heavy barge traffic. Temporary mooring to await the lock opening is, of course, necessary and it is for this reason that permanent mooring is prohibited.

As explained previously, it is imperative that you moor, facing upstream or into the tide. Not only is it easier to bring your craft alongside a berth under proper control but it will also be far easier when leaving. On a canal this consideration is not so important, of course, since in most cases there is little current except near locks or where the canal is used as a feeder for a water undertaking. Also you should remember that with most cruisers and definitely all narrow boats of seventy feet you can only turn at a proper winding hole.

Mooring stern-on to a quay may be necessary in crowded anchorages such as are found on the Broads in the height of the season. The basic method shown in Fig. 52 will probably have to be adapted if you are to lie alongside other craft. Make sure the craft upstream of you is adequately secured to take your lines and, as an added precaution use your anchor or mud-weight as a secondary 'kedge' off your bow on the upstream side. This type of mooring is only possible where there is plenty of width in the stream and tide or current effects are small.

BASIC METHODS
In the last section we dealt with the various hitches to be used for mooring purposes. It pays to have the crew practise tying these knots as often as possible, not only so that the boat will be properly secured but so that any other member of the crew will know how to untie it.

For convenience, Fig. 15 is repeated here at Fig. 51 as the basic terms applicable to mooring ropes are shown and described in greater detail. The nomenclature of these ropes may differ slightly, especially in the descriptions of the springs, in various parts of the country. However, it is important to remember, whatever else anyone calls it, that a forespring is one which is secured at a point on the quay in front of, or forward of its point of attachment to the vessel. A backspring, conversely is where the point on the quay is behind the point of attachment on the vessel. Further descriptions are sometimes applied, depending on the point of attachment on the vessel; thus a forward backspring would be the term applied to that shown in the figure, since the cleat is forward of a line drawn amidships. An after backspring would start from a cleat aft and run further aft but should not be confused with the stern rope which is carried ashore and secured well behind the stern whereas the backspring would normally be secured ashore level with or forward of the stern.

All six ropes can be used for a really secure mooring in canals and rivers which are not subject to changes in level. Where such changes are likely, and a member of the crew will not be tending the lines, the breast ropes should not be set up. Obviously, for mooring in tidal waters, unless to a floating pontoon, or where changes in level do occur, springs, head and stern ropes should be as long as possible if the craft is to be left for an appreciable period.

Fig. 52 shows a suggested method of mooring 'Stern-On' to a quay where there is sufficient depth of water. Always check this latter point first. If in any doubt, make up an improvised lead line to plumb the depth. This is quite easily done before you set off with some stout cord and a suitable weight. The old-fashioned pound weight will suffice admirably, although the approved lead is of 7 lb. and has a hollow in the base for greasing when the composition of the river or sea-bed requires to be checked. A cord is attached and the first couple of fathoms marked at half fathom intervals, thereafter marking can be continued in the approved nautical fashion as shown in the

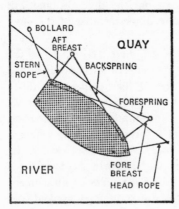

Fig. 51. Mooring rope terms

accompanying chart, (Fig. 53). If the line is going to be used, always with the same craft, it is a good idea to make a permanent marking of your 'safe depth' which should be equal to the draft of the vessel plus between one half and one quarter of that amount. A fathom equals six feet.

FATHOMS	MARKINGS
$\frac{1}{2}$	A single knot in the line
1	1 strip of leather
$1\frac{1}{2}$	2 knots, 1 in. apart
2	2 strips of leather
3	3 strips of leather
5	1 piece of white calico, etc.
etc.	

Fig. 53.
Lead line marking

Fig. 54 shows the method of mooring where the river bed slopes gradually away from the bank, giving shallow water close inshore. The bow is virtually beached while the sterngear is allowed to ride clear out in deeper water. The shear of the bow should be brought as close to the bank as possible and held there tightly by short breast and head ropes. Check that the level is not likely to drop or rise if leaving the boat for a long period. The forespring is now set up to prevent the stern swinging too far out and into the path of passing craft. This method can also be used against a weedy shore.

Hire firms tend to be rather cheeseparing with the amount and number of mooring lines granted per boat. The usual complement is three warps. The foregoing diagrams, therefore will have to be followed with some thought as to what can safely be left out. Correctly moored against the current as in Fig. 51, it will be observed, if we ignore the breast ropes, that only two ropes are actually in tension, the others merely acting to keep the boat alongside the bank or quay. These are the bow – or headrope and the forespring. It may be possible to use the inboard end of the headrope to form a forward breast rope by passing a hitch round the bow cleat and taking the end ashore as shown. The third warp should be used to form the stern rope to keep the stern in, or if a forward breast rope is inadvisable through tidal or current level changes, the back-

117

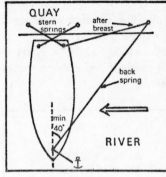

Fig. 52. Mooring stern to quay

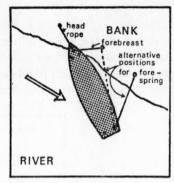

Fig. 54. Mooring to shallow shore

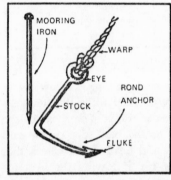

Fig. 55. Mooring iron and Rond Anchor

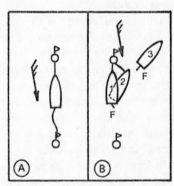

Fig. 56. Clearing a mooring with dominant wind ahead
(a) Moored fore and aft
(b) Stern moorings dropped

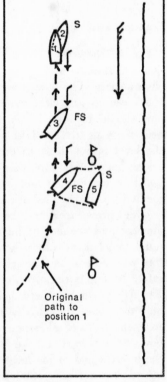

Fig. 57. Mooring in a dominant head wind

spring should be set up to prevent the bow paying off. Fig. 54, is really a modification of the above principle and, of course, needs no adaptation since it only requires three warps in any case.

Mooring irons of the crowbar type should be driven into the bank by means of the sledge hammer provided, set at an angle of about 20 degrees out of the vertical away from the craft. This prevents a fairly thick rope which may not give a very tight hitch, riding up the post, pulling it over, or slipping off altogether. Drive the iron well in but not so far that to release it will be difficult nor so that a short stump appears above your hitch. To release, merely heave the top of the iron horizontally into the vertical and back again a few times and it will then be found it can be withdrawn quite easily.

Rond anchors (Fig. 55) are a common sight on the Broads. Despite their title they should *not* be used for anchor work. But they do provide a quick method for securing mooring lines ashore, and can usually be secured by placing the spiked end in the ground and then tramping it in by means of striking the stock with the heel or a blunt instrument. To release, lift the stock near the eye and then heave until the spike is loose enough to be withdrawn. The holding power of a rond anchor is not as high as that of the iron stake, and in soft or marshy ground it will tend to drag. Always use a bollard, if one is handy or the mooring rings supplied at recognised mooring places. If the rond anchor is permanently attached to its warp the mooring hitch shown on Fig. 42, should be used.

FLOATING MOORINGS
We will now deal briefly with the clearing and picking up of the floating mooring. This consists, either of a buoy which is attached by chains to ground tackle on the bed of the river, having a mooring ring provided on the buoy or a marker float which must be brought aboard with its line at the end of which a proper mooring chain is attached. Either pattern is anchored by a concrete weight singly or may be fastened in line with others to a ground chain weighted at both ends. The latter method of laying is termed a 'trot'. The procedure for mooring to a pile driven into the river bed off-shore is also similar and the following remarks can easily be adopted for this situation.

119

No hard and fast rule can be given about the holding power of a mooring buoy. Naturally it varies according to strength of current and in tidal waters, the holding power tends to alter with the rise and fall of the tide. A note of the size of craft on adjacent moorings should be a reasonable guide, but make sure that it is a mooring buoy you are picking up! Floats for race markers, fishing nets, lobster pots and other people's anchors have all been seized on before now and havoc caused as a result. MAKE SURE IT IS WHAT YOU THINK IT IS AND ALSO THAT YOU WILL BE PERMITTED TO USE IT!!!

Many moorings are laid by private individuals or clubs and, apart from the original cost, charges are levied on them by the navigation authority. Make sure that you can use the mooring first. Only in cases of dire and obvious emergency is it wise to use first and ask afterwards, for it is often true that a courteous request will gain you valuable assistance in the matter, whereas the silent assumption that 'it'll be all right as long as we move if the owner turns up' leads to frayed tempers, righteous indignation on the part of the owner or lessee, and bad feeling all round.

A safety point on mid-stream mooring or anchoring is worth noting here. It is a good idea to secure a life-line from fore to aft on both sides of the hull so that it lies against the topsides within easy reach of a swimmer or a crew member who may have inadvertently missed his footing and fallen into the water. It is also useful when boarding ship from the dinghy.

CLEARING

You will probably find it helpful to re-read pages 36 and 39 on the subject of wind and current effects, since these are most important to understand if you are to clear and pick up a mooring successfully.

Remember that a craft at rest will tend to swing head to wind or head to current or tide if moored or anchored at the bow, depending on which of these two elements is the 'dominant' one. Once released, she will come broadside on to the wind, a factor which is often of assistance in clearing a buoy. A strong current, too, will tend to carry the vessel away from a buoy once it is released, useful no doubt, but extremely galling if someone has had to climb on to the buoy to release the lines and thereby becomes stranded!

To avoid the necessity of crew members being cast adrift in this way the best method of attachment to a buoy we have found is merely to pass a loop through the mooring ring, retaining both ends of the warp on board the cruiser. The mooring can then be 'slipped' as the nautical expression implies, by releasing one end and allowing it to pass through the ring as the cruiser moves off. Note that when allowing a line to slip through a ring, the end that comes away from the underside of the ring should be pulled, since tension on top of the ring may jam the line altogether. Make sure the 'pull' lifts the ring.

Before slipping the mooring, start the engine. Check wind and current directions carefully and, as far as possible, decide whether the wind or current is the dominant factor in relation to your craft, or whether neither is sufficient to warrant consideration.

For a motor cruiser of the type we are considering, broadly speaking tide or current must be virtually slack and the wind speed somewhere below Force 3 (7 knots) for either effect to be discounted.

Follow the directions given below and note that if your craft has been middled between two buoys, i.e. ahead and astern, always cast off stern first and except where specifically mentioned, haul up to the buoy ahead in order to clear that astern.

If it is decided that wind and current can be ignored, i.e. that it is calm, drop your mooring or slip the line as the case may be and go astern with the helm amidships. The stern will swing to port and the vessel gradually gather way sternwards off the mooring. When clear, go ahead on course. A word about dropping a mooring – never walk along the deck with the marker, thinking that you will ensure its clearance by casting it aft, having let the chain go. It is imperative that chain, line and marker are all got rid of at the same time, preferably from the bow if that was the point of attachment. If you had also been secured aft, remember the rule, that you must cast off the stern mooring first.

With a dominant current, having slipped your mooring, put your helm to starboard and allow the craft to drift off. Then, putting your helm to port, engage forward gear and steam clear.

If you are starting from between two buoys, let go aft first, haul up to the forward mooring before slipping it. It is imperative that your engine is running and warmed up before you attempt to clear any mooring, either floating, or where you are berthed to a quay or the river bank.

A dominant wind is much more common with a power cruiser, having a shallow draft and extensive cabin and wheelhouse accommodation. Do not therefore assume that because an ocean-going yacht, moored close to you, lies in a particular way that this is an indication of the circumstances that apply to your own vessel. Being deep-keeled and with a low superstructure she is probably much more dependent on the current or tide than you are for a position, and it may need a much stronger blow to overcome the effects of the current on her hull compared with yours.

With the wind ahead, put the wheel over in either direction and give a short kick ahead on the engine, paying the bow mooring line out at the same time so that the wind will be brought on to the beam. Then slip the mooring line and steam off. Make sure that the line does not trail in the water and so foul the propeller. If you are between two buoys, you will, of course, follow the same routine, having cast your stern line off before putting the wheel over and engaging the gear.

If you are moored between two buoys it is likely that you may find yourself with a dominant wind aft or on the beam to start off with. It is highly unlikely that this will occur if you are only moored to one buoy, for obvious reasons.

With the wind aft, slacken the stern rope and allow the ship to blow off so that the wind comes on to the quarter. Then go astern, taking the head rope in so that, as the vessel gathers way, it swings to seek the wind. As you pass the stern mooring buoy, cut the engine, take in the stern line and continue astern until well clear.

If the wind is on the beam, you will need plenty of room to manoeuvre to leeward. Let go the stern line and wait for the vessel to swing until she comes up head to wind on the forward mooring. Then proceed as before as for the headwind manoeuvre in the previous paragraph but one.

PICKING UP MOORINGS

DO NOT 'FINISH WITH ENGINES' until you are SECURELY MOORED. This is most important.

Where the wind and current are comparatively calm, picking up a mooring can be tricky. Approach the buoy slowly so that it comes fine on the starboard bow. To stop, you will have to engage 'reverse' and this action should swing the bow on to the buoy so that it can be picked up. If your swing comes too early and the buoy is missed, keep in reverse for a reasonable distance and approach again.

If you have to moor to two buoys in these conditions, i.e. one ahead and one astern, ignore the stern buoy until you are secured by the bow and then try and drift the cruiser back by paying out the head rope, until the buoy astern can be reached. Then 'middle' the vessel between the two buoys. Failure to 'middle' a vessel in this way can set up rather an unpleasant motion in a strong wind and especially in a tideway.

With a dominant stream, picking up a mooring is easier, as long as you remember to use the braking effect of the stream and do not have to resort to reversing your propeller to take way off. Approach with the buoy fine on the PORT bow, since you have been advised not to use reverse, holding the vessel slowly against the current until movement over the ground is almost imperceptible. A short kick ahead will swing the bow to port on to the buoy and it can be picked up. Keep moving slightly forward to ease the strain as the mooring line is threaded or the float brought aboard. The boat hook again is a useful implement here. When secured and only when – cut the engine. If by some ghastly mischance you overshoot the buoy, allow the vessel to drift back and make the approach again. Going round in circles in a crowded anchorage only advertises your mistake!!

With a dominant wind ahead, things become tricky. Pass upwind of the buoy, leaving it to STARBOARD. When well clear, put the helm over to starboard so that a swing is started in that direction to bring the wind on to the Port bow and allow the vessel to drift back with the helm kept over to Port. Short kicks ahead on the engine will keep the bow towards the wind until the buoy is passed when a final burst ahead will bring the buoy inside on the port bow where it can be picked up. Once secured, cut the engine. (Fig. 57)

An easier method is to pass upwind of the buoy, leaving it to port and when clear, put out a 'kedge' from the bow and disengage gear. Dredge back by putting the helm to port in a similar manner to that described under the 'Engine Stall' emergency procedure described on page 60, dragging the kedge. Give a final kick ahead when the buoy is level with the stern to bring it alongside the port bow. Secure your head rope or pick up the buoy and secure to the mooring chain to which it is attached.

If using a kedge in this way it is advisable to use it with a trip line and float. The line is fastened to the crown ring of the anchor and a marker float attached to the other end of the line. In crowded anchorages the anchor chain may easily foul a mooring or the flukes of the anchor be caught in another vessel's lines or mooring trots. In these cases the main kedge anchor chain must be unshackled from the inboard end and let go while the marker and line are hauled in followed by the anchor and its chain. This should be done, obviously, from the opposite side of the obstruction if this can be reasonably determined.

Hire cruisers are not normally provided with the refinements of a separate kedge anchor, or for that matter, a trip line and float so that if a kedging operation is to be attempted, a warp should be temporarily made up to the anchor supplied (or mudweight), with a one gallon oil can (well stoppered!) or a spare fender as a float. The length of line should be such that the warp is equal in length to the depth of water in which the operation is to be carried out. Check this with your homemade lead line.

WINDING SHIP

When describing the manoeuvring of craft when berthing we impressed readers with the necessity of mooring, facing upstream. It is admitted that in tidal waters, that while this may be possible when berthing it may be necessary to leave a berth when the tide has turned and to facilitate a seamanlike clearance of the berth it may be advisable to turn the ship at the quay before departing. This manoeuvre is known as 'winding ship' and is effected quite simply as follows, provided that the wind is not too strong.

A line is run from the offshore bow cleat, round the stem and back up the quay side of the vessel to a bollard on the quay at about the usual point the forward backspring would be secured. The same bollard can, of course, be used. This line is left slack, all lines except the forward backspring being taken in. This latter line is therefore now taking all the strain. For assistance in the manoeuvre the engine should be started and kept running as it will probably be needed as described.

The stream coming astern will now ease the stern out, but if not, put the helm towards the quay and give a short kick ahead with the engine. During the swing, an occasional kick astern with the engine will stop the bow from fouling on the quay and damaging quay or paintwork on your craft.

When the vessel is at right angles to the quay, slacken off the backspring and harden in the other line, fastened to the offshore bow cleat so that it snubs the bow in towards the position formerly occupied by the stern. A little forward power will bring the vessel back into her original position but reversed and ready to clear the berth in the approved manner, facing into the current. If the departure is not immediate, set up the headrope, springs and stern rope again.

It sometimes happens that you decide to venture up a little-used waterway or one that has no special turning point at its limit of navigation. In either case you may decide that it would be advisable to avoid executing a short-round turn under power in mid-stream, perhaps due to the restricted room and/or set of the current. A controlled turn from the bank is obviously the answer on similar lines to those described above. However, having arrived upstream, to 'wind ship' in this case the procedure will have to be reversed.

A line is set up from the offshore quarter of the craft. There may be no cleat, so that a rail stanchion or fender eye may have to be used, but only if such fitting is a substantial one since the weight of the cruiser as taken by the current is going to be checked on this one rope.

The rope is passed round the stern and should be stopped with twine on the stern cleats to prevent it dropping and fouling the propeller or rudder during the manoeuvre. It is thence taken forward up the shore side of the craft to a convenient point on the bank, approximately level with the centre of the craft. Start the engine but DO NOT ON ANY ACCOUNT engage the gears.

Slip all forward lines first and push out the bow. Slip any remaining stern lines except the control line set up. The stream should now take the vessel right round and the stern should be fended from the bank or quay with adequate fend-offs or even coir matting if any is available. The line from the quarter should now be tensioned and the cruiser's position controlled by means of the engine and a judicious fend off at the bow. A line thrown from the bow can be secured and the necessary mooring lines set up before switching off the engine.

Remember that if current and wind permit, do not be frightened of manhandling a power cruiser at moorings. Although slow, the degree of control you have over a cruiser's movement is infinitely more precise if handled by line than if under power.

SUMMARY

1. Always moor facing upstream or so that the bow will stem the tide.
2. In tidal waters or where the river or canal level is liable to fluctuate use springs or, better still head and stern ropes. Springs should not be used without a head and stern rope. On no account use breast ropes unless the lines are to be constantly tended.
3. Make sure that you are not breaking the law!
4. If a mooring is to be made elsewhere than at a recognised mooring place and there is sufficient depth of water, a spot should be chosen where obstruction is unlikely to be caused.
5. Do not moor so that you obstruct channel markers or buoys.
6. Check as to whether you are required to show lights at night while moored. In most commercial waterways you must conform to the bye-laws in this respect, which usually require the exhibition of a white light visible all round from the forepart of the vessel.
7. See also the section on anchor work for mooring in tidal waters.
8. Check the safe depth under your keel.

SECTION VIII

ANCHOR WORK

Canal Anchoring
Types of Anchor
Basic Anchoring
Weighing Anchor
Anchoring in Tidal Waters
(For other uses of the Anchor – See pages 52, 60, 115 and 124).

Illustrations

SECTION VIII

ANCHOR WORK

Before outlining the principles of anchor work we should stress that it is extremely unwise to anchor in a canal. There may even be bye-laws or regulations preventing the use of the anchor. Check first. Many canals which do not follow a natural watercourse (some, of course, do, being canalised rivers, termed in France – 'racles') are constructed on made up ground or through geological strata which demand a waterproof skin to the bed, known as 'puddling'. An anchor may easily damage the puddling, permitting a leak of the canal water which, at worst, could dry out of that particular 'pound' as each section between locks is called. A mudweight (D' in Fig. 58) does not invite the same criticism, and, although of little use on a hard bed, most canals are sufficiently silted these days to provide enough ooze to hold the mudweight down.

* * *

The use of the anchor has already been discussed in connection with turning, emergency handling and mooring. As far as inland waterway work is concerned it has only really one other use and that is its primary function for providing a temporary mooring where no provision has been made in the waterway by means of trots or mooring tackle or it is not possible to moor to the bank or a quay.

The patterns most commonly used are the C.Q.R. (E) or Danforth (F) anchors, since these, for their weight, have superior holding powers to the old pattern of Fisherman (A) or the stockless anchor which is popular in larger ships since it can be hauled into the hawsepipe and retained there. Small craft are sometimes equipped with a grapnel (B) but these are fearsome implements to stow unless of the folding type. Where the river bed is formed of soft mud, as on the Broads, a mudweight (as shown in Fig. 58 at D) can be used. It is easy to stow and, in the conditions it is designed for, quite effective.

128

The anchor should be equipped with a warp, in length at least five times the maximum depth in which you plan to cruise, taking into account the highest river level or tide you may encounter. Do not be mislead by the maximum dimensions of craft that can be accommodated on a waterway as published by the relevant authority. This of course has to relate to the *minimum* measurements of the channel, dictated by a structure such as a lock, aqueduct, tunnel or bridge. For instance, a maximum draft of 4 feet 6 inches for a craft indicates that the depth runs from about 5 feet *upwards* and in some cases could be as much as 15 feet or more. The warp may be of rope or chain, but if of rope, the anchor end should have a length of chain leading from the anchor ring for about eight to twelve feet before the rope starts. This is to ensure that, when dropped, the anchor lies correctly to engage with the bed, as will be described later.

It is a wise precaution also to provide a trip line and float, the length of the trip line equalling the greatest depth in which

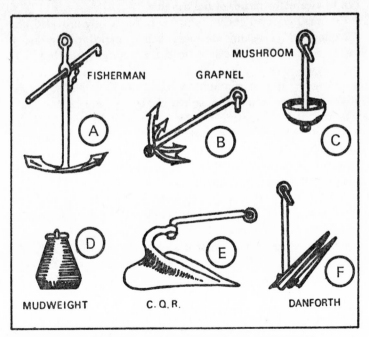

Fig. 58. Common types of anchor for small craft

129

you will anchor and made up of a rope of sufficient strength not to part from the anchor if it is desired to haul in the anchor and main chain or warp by means of it. Proper floats can be obtained for this purpose, provided with a handle for getting aboard but if you have to make up your own use a well stoppered empty gallon can or one of the buoyant types of fend-offs, usually supplied with a cruiser. The trip line is attached to the 'crown' or base of the stem of the anchor by means of a clove hitch or where a ring is provided for this purpose, a fishermen's bend.

The anchor should be kept on deck in the bow, if possible cradled in some kind of brackets or lashed to the deck. It is permanently attached to the warp which is lead through a chain pipe down into the chain locker or forepeak, which is the first space in the boat below the deck behind the stem. The chain or warp should be flaked down in the locker, but make certain that the inboard fastening can easily be reached so that in the event of a foul anchor, it can be unfastened so that the anchor can be cleared by means of the trip line.

On small craft an anchor winch is not normally provided, the fastening and checking on deck being carried out round a samson post which is built in to the structure of the boat. Do not rely on deck cleats which may be only screwed to the deck boarding or at best through to the thwarts or beams. In the absence of a samson post a bolted cleat may be used, but make sure that it will take the weight required of it, and watch for any sign of lift after the anchor has been laid. When passing the anchor over the bow, pay the warp out over a fairlead and not over the rail which will easily be damaged and will soon chafe a rope warp apart.

Fig. 60 shows the method of securing the anchor once the correct length of warp has been paid out. Check the position and depth in which you propose to anchor, and, bearing in mind the factors of wind and current and which element will be the dominant one, approach from the position in which the craft will eventually rest, i.e. downstream or downwind. When over the spot, disengage gear, let go the anchor and trip line and buoy, and pay out three times the depth on the warp, allowing the vessel to drop astern. To facilitate checking on the length of warp, it should, of course be marked. Usual practice dictates marking every five fathoms, but for river work, you may find it better to mark each fathom – one band for one fathom, two for two, changing colour at five and again at ten and so on. A chain is usually marked by painting, and with luck a rope will take paint if carefully applied.

Watch the warp and when it appears to tauten, check by observing the bank or some object on shore whether the vessel's drift has stopped or if she still appears to be dragging the anchor. If the dragging does not cease, you will have to steam up to the anchor, break it out and try anchoring again in a more favourable spot.

Anchors are so designed to break out (lift from the river bed) when the warp extends vertically to the surface. To engage with the bed the stem has to lie horizontally along the bed. It is for this reason that the weight of the chain helps in bringing the stem down, the stock of the fisherman anchor in particular assisting the flukes to engage. As soon as the vessel drops astern, therefore, the chain begins to pull the anchor over on to the bed and it should engage as soon as the drag of the vessel tautens the chain.

The normal length of warp, if of chain should, as explained, be three times the depth. If of rope you may have to increase this to five times. In strong tidal waters or in high winds even a chain warp should be increased to this figure to stop the vessel dragging. Chain, for an anchor warp, should always be used since rope tends to lift and so drag the anchor more easily.

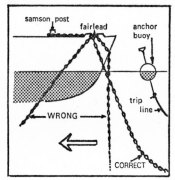

Fig. 59. Anchor chain position

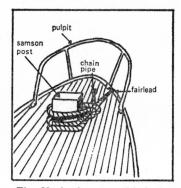

Fig. 60. Anchor warp hitched to samson post

131

When required to raise the anchor, steam up to it and as soon as the warp grows straight down, start hauling in. The anchor should now break out. To raise without a winch, take one or two turns round the samson post as shown in Fig. 61, and, snubbing the rope or chain with the palm of the left hand, fingers well clear! take a snatch with the right hand when conditions permit. It is better, of course, to employ more than one member of the crew, but make sure that they use the fairlead and all remain well inboard. A look-out should be posted in the bow, unconnected with the hauling party to signal when the anchor has broken the surface, so that the topsides will not be damaged and the anchor can be got safely aboard. Do not forget to collect the trip line and buoy, if attached, at the same time.

If there is a lot of movement in the anchorage it may be found that the anchor warp keeps tightening over the fairlead, incurring an intermittent chafing which should be avoided at all costs, especially with modern nylon ropes which it has been found, can be considerably weakened by friction heat being generated in the strands. The best cure is to make up a kind of shock absorber, which consists of a weight fastened to a loop, which is passed round the warp and lowered down it to an extent of about half the scope of the warp. This will take any slack out of the warp and ensure a permanent positioning of the warp in the fairlead.

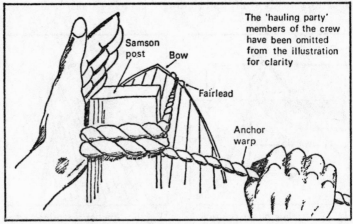

Fig. 61. Getting in the anchor

In tidal waters, if the tide is to turn while you are anchored, make sure that you will not foul any other craft on the turn and be ready to deal with your own anchor which may start to drag. Even if it does not, your chain may wrap itself round the unused fluke, if you are using the conventional pattern of fisherman anchor, and you will have to be prepared to raise it by means of the trip line, if it does not break out by the usual method.

It is therefore safer and more advisable to anchor to two bower anchors if you have them aboard. This considerably reduces the radius of swing when the tide turns and provided all other craft are so anchored it means that many more craft can be safely anchored in a given area. Figs. 62 and 63 below will readily show why it is more preferable to adopt this method. In addition, it ensures that a secondary anchor is provided should the other, for any reason fail. A well-found cruiser, which is likely to cruise in estuary or coastal waters should always possess more than one anchor. The holding power of the second need not be for the full weight of the cruiser, so that it might be possible to provide a 'C.Q.R.' for the main anchor and a 'Fisherman' of the same weight (less holding power) as the secondary anchor which would be slightly cheaper in initial cost.

This second anchor might conveniently be kept near the stern of the craft until required, as in certain circumstances of an emergency nature it can be used from the stern to assist in

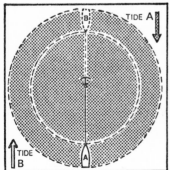

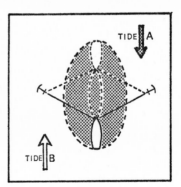

Fig. 62. Single anchoring   Fig. 63. Double anchoring

Note the hatched areas required for movement of the craft with the tide turning or holding the stern in which large craft are passing in a restricted channel.

When anchoring with two anchors from the bow, drop the main anchor first as described, but when backing off, pay out twice as much scope as is required. Let go the second anchor with a little more warp than is required for its final 'scope'. Now move ahead up to the first anchor again, taking in its scope and letting out the warp further at the same rate for the second anchor. When middled between the two anchors fasten the secondary warp to the primary anchor chain and let go so that they sink to the river bed.

Always weigh the secondary anchor first when leaving the mooring, by reversing this procedure. Do NOT forget to provide both anchors with their own trip lines.

SECTION IX

RUNNING THE SHIP

Coming Aboard
Clothing
Food and Stores
Writing Up the Log
Simple Meteorology
Sea and Chemical Toilets
Water Supplies
Gas Appliances
Electrical Appliances
Fire Prevention
Towing and Using the Dinghy

Illustrations

SECTION IX

RUNNING THE SHIP

Before welcoming your crew aboard, they usually appreciate a personal letter from you, detailing what they should and what they should not bring with them. The authors duplicated a set of notes to send each prospective crew member and these form the basis of the notes on clothing below. Provisioning a boat can also be a bit of a headache but it is extremely unwise and also bad for morale to set sail without any food aboard. The excuse that the organiser of a cruise is not aware of his shipmates' eating habits is a lame one, since, after a morning's back-breaking work in the fresh air negotiating four or five locks, most crew will have forgotten any fads and fancies they may have about food. Plain cooking is best, unless, of course, you have a 'Cordon Bleu' aboard.

With half a dozen or more aboard, it is advisable to split the crew in half into two watches, 'A' and 'B' or 'Port' and 'Starboard' to give the watches a more nautical title, which is nowadays only salutary since it rarely has anything to do with the parts of the ship. Originally it stemmed from the locations of the particular watches' quarters. Each watch is commanded by a qualified master or helmsman if possible and, for inland waterways purposes where it is proposed only to run in daylight hours a watch can last for four hours, change of watch being made at around midday.

CLOTHING
Tidiness aboard a small boat is essential. If you arrive with trunks and suitcases, unpack them immediately, using the locker and cupboard space available. Non-folding luggage should either be locked in your car ashore or left in the care of the boatyard before getting under way.

It is suggested that proper yachting shoes are worn. Dunlop produce a specially treaded sole and heel type of plimsoll called a 'Magister' yachting shoe at approximately £2. Cheaper shoes of this type by other manufacturers are also available, are just as effective and cost from about £1 upwards. Some yachtsmen prefer ankle boots. These are waterproof but obviously heavier. Crêpe and multicellular rubber soles and heels are lethal on a wet deck (or a dry painted or metal one for that matter). Rope sandals are a good and cheaper substitute but if all else fails the safest standby is bare feet!

Proper waterproof outerwear and a hat are a must; plenty of woollies, jeans (two pairs if possible) and, for the men, a blazer, flannels, soft shirt and tie for evening sorties, while the ladies will probably find jumpers or blouses and skirts or slacks are easier to keep tidy in the confined storage space of a boat.

It cannot be emphasised too strongly that a supply of socks will be appreciated by the wearer, especially if wet weather is encountered. Half-a-dozen pairs for a week should be regarded as a minimum, even though washing facilities will no doubt present themselves.

Two towels per person, at least, are advisable and do not forget flannel, tooth equipment, soap and razor. Most boats have only a 12 volt (occasionally 24 volt) electricity supply, so that unless you have been advised that there is an AC inverter aboard, power razors not rated at the lower voltages will be white elephants on your trip.

It should also be stressed to your crew that they are advised to bring sun-glasses with them. It can be most disconcerting, trying to steer with the sun reflecting off the water.

Basically, try to dress for comfort rather than high fashion.

SUGGESTED PACKING LISTS

LADIES

1 Windcheater or heavy pull-over.
1 Woollen or plastic hat.
7 Changes underwear.
1 pr. Shorts, slacks or jeans.
1 Swim suit.
1 Cardigan.
2 Skirts.
1 Sewing outfit.

1 Plastic Raincoat
1 pr. Yachting or rope-soled shoes.
1 pr. Shoes.
3 prs. Stockings.
2 prs. Ankle socks.
2 Towels.
2 or 3 Blouses.

GENTLEMEN

2 Windcheaters or pullovers.	6 prs. Socks.
1 Woollen, plastic or oilskin hat.	1 pr. Yachting or rope-soled shoes.
7 Changes underwear.	1 Blazer.
2 or 3 Comfortable soft shirts.	1 pr. Flannels.
2 Tee shirts.	1 pr. Sandals or shoes.
2 prs. Jeans or slacks.	2 Ties.
1 pr. Swim trunks.	2 Towels.
1 pr. Oilskins or GOOD waterproof.	1 Razor.

FOOD

We have taken an example of one of our own cruises which run from Friday night to Sunday afternoon, usually accommodating 10 to 14 people on two or more cruisers. The stores are delivered to the boats, a practice popular and well organised on the Broads and Thames by grocers local to the boatyard. Payment is made, either direct or through the yard.

Private owners can, of course, make similar arrangements or pick up their order from their local grocer for transfer to the boat with the rest of their luggage by car.

The idea is to work out your menu first and then go through it carefully abstracting the individual items required to make up that menu. It is useless to try and order a lot of food with vague thoughts at the back of your mind as to when you might use it. If you don't happen to be the family housekeeper and you are asked to feed a crew, here is what we suggest.

We use preprinted order forms which we compiled for the cruising section of the Club to which we belong. These are filled in and supplied to the grocer for delivery aboard on the Friday afternoon. Riverside grocers often produce their own forms and a number of boatyards will as well. These avoid items being overlooked since they list pretty well all that you will need. The Club's form is divided into sections so that if necessary, say, Butchery, Bakery and Greengrocery items can be detached and ordered from another store or shop.

Milk sometimes presents storage and availability problems, especially if there is no fridge. Some hire firms provide ice-boxes which can be recharged, a practice prevalent on the Broads. Longlife milk is now available in cartons and is designed to keep for a matter of weeks after purchase. It costs about 1d. per pint more than ordinary milk. Alternatively you can reduce your milk order and use such proprietary powdered milks as 'Milac' or 'Marvel' which, to most people, are perfectly acceptable, even on cornflakes.

'Smash' or 'Yeoman' potato powders are easier to carry and store but expensive. Fresh vegetables are preferable and usually cheaper than tinned or frozen, when in season.

Tins, bottles and galley refuse should never be thrown overboard even if there is no prohibition in effect (which there is on the Thames) since it is not unknown for a soggy tin label to have found its way into the engine's water circulating system and blocked the inlet strainer. Even if it doesn't block yours, it might block that of the next passing cruiser.

WEEK-END MENU (10 – 14 CREW)

Friday Evening
Soup
Bacon, Eggs,
Beans & Tomatoes
Cake
Tea

Saturday Morning
Tea
Cornflakes
Sausage & Eggs
Toast & Marmalade
Tea & Coffee
Coffee & Biscuits

Saturday Noon
Steak & Kidney Pie
Peas, Mashed Potatoes &
Gravy.
Fruit Salad & Cream
Tea

Saturday Evening
Shepherd's Pie,
Brussels & Mashed.
Fruit Tart & Custard
Coffee

Sunday Morning
Tea
Cornflakes
Scrambled Eggs
Toast & Marmalade
Tea & Coffee
Coffee & Biscuits

Sunday Noon
Soup
Roast Beef or Lamb
Cabbage & Potato
Fruit Salad & Cream.
Coffee

Sunday Afternoon
Jam Doorsteps or Cake.
Tea

To provide this menu see next page for list of stores required.

STORES LIST compiled from foregoing Menu :

½ lb. Tea	4 tins Fruit	*Washing up liquid
1 lge. Instant Coffee	4 small Cream	*Dish Cloth
4 lb. Sugar	4 lge. Soup	*Scrubber
1½ lb. Butter	1 lb. Marmalade	*Tea Towels
15 pts. Milk	1 lb. Jam	*2 Toilet Rolls
3 doz. Eggs	2 pt. pkts. Custard	*Brasso
2 lb. Bacon	2 lb. Asst. Biscuits	*Dusters
4 lb. Meat	2 Fruit tarts	*Matches
2 Cabbages	1½ lb. Cake	
2 lb. Sausages	2 lb. Mince	*These items ob-
1 lb. Brussels	2 Steak Pies	viously apply in
1½ lb. Peas	1½ lb. Tomatoes	all cases and
14 lb. Potatoes	1 lge. Baked Beans	should not be
1 lge. Cornflakes	1 Gravy Powder	overlooked.
3 lge. Loaves	Salt, pepper, etc.	
1 small Cocoa	1 Bot. Cooking Oil	

WRITING UP THE LOG

An important part of running the ship is the keeping of a log. Most authorities on the subject like to leave the amateur yachtsman in the slough of 'personal preference' especially with regard to inland waterways and even coastal navigation. This is a load of bunkum. FOR THE KEEPING OF A LOG ON AN INLAND WATERWAY THERE SHOULD BE A MINIMUM ACCEPTABLE STANDARD of what should be included.

A log should indicate the taking on of fuel and oil especially important on a motor cruiser, and water; engine servicing requirements and performance can then readily be ascertained and water consumption and storage are vital to the comfort and efficiency of the crew. Weather forecasts and prevailing condititions should be carefully noted and for ease of entry the Beaufort Notation can be used. Some common examples are given in the article following on Simple Meteorology.

Most chandlers sell log books, but these are usually only glorified exercise books and a good log book is best ruled up on a cash book which has been turned upside down so that the cash columns come at the left-hand side of the page. Our club devised its own ruling, which is a fairly basic one, but an even simpler one used by the Island Cruising Club of Salcombe is also shown which uses the inverted single column cash book without amendment. Stiff backed books of this type are readily and cheaply obtainable from most Woolworth stores.

CRAFT					DATE				
TIME	COURSE	LOG	SPEED	FUEL	MET	WIND		BAR	REMARKS
						D	F		

Fig. 65. Ruling designed for sail and power cruising

TIME	COURSE	WIND	LOG	REMARKS	BAR

Fig. 66. Inverted 'cash book' ruling

The items shown in Fig. 65, not having specific columns allotted to them in Fig. 66 are written in the rather larger remarks column of the latter but the following remarks apply equally to the method of compiling your log.

The columns are arranged so that fairly rapid calculations can be made when assessing speed, a useful factor for working out estimated times of arrival. To this must be added a constant of say, 15 minutes per lock, multiplied by the number of locks you will have to negotiate before reaching your destination. Waiting time will also have to be taken into account in busy periods. The remarks columns can be used for narrative of sightings, incidents aboard and alterations of course. An example is given overleaf.

COURSE
Inland cruises need merely show the direction proceeded along a channel such as 'Upstream' or 'Downstream', or 'Towards –' followed by the name of the next major town. This applies particularly in relation to canals.

You may well ask why it is necessary to keep a log. As already mentioned it is a considerable aid to engine servicing of a power cruiser, it ensures that items of importance are not overlooked, and it should be remembered that in the event of an

141

TIME	COURSE	LOG	SPEED	FUEL	MET.	WIND		BAR.	REMARKS
						D	F		
1000	Upstream	0		20	d	SW	4	—	Left Bates' yard
1015									Left Chertsey lock
1035		2			o				Arrived Penton Hook
1045									Left Penton Hook
1115		3½	3½		o	SW	4		Arrived Staines and moored for provisions
1145		3½			o				Left Staines
1210		5							Cleared Bell Weir
1245		7½	4						Cleared Old Windsor after a contretemps with the dinghy
1300		9¼	6½		d	SW	2		Passed Datchet
1315		10¾							Entered Romney lock
1320									Cleared Romney lock
1330		11							Arrived Windsor Quay
1500		11							Left Windsor Quay
1525		13	4						Cleared Boveney lock
1605		16	4½						Arrived Bray lock
1650		18	3		r	SW	2		Moored off Boulters and shipped dinghy
1705		18			r				Cleared Boulters
1730		20½	6						Cleared Cookham lock
1745		21	2	14	r				Moored up at Steamer jetty at Cookham

Fig. 67. Log of m/v 'Shaula Star' 14.10.67. River Thames

142

accident a full report will have to be submitted to the insurers. How much easier this will be with a well kept log at hand!

If canal cruising, matters requiring the attention of the water-way authority should also be reported from your records as these bodies are usually short-staffed and appreciate constructive advice such as the presence of excessive weed, locks out of order, banks in need of attention and so on.

SIMPLE METEOROLOGY

In the last article on the log-book we glossed over the matters affecting the weather since we intend to deal with these in more detail now. Wind direction and force can only be recorded from careful observation. The method of determining the wind force however, is usually described in the Almanacs in relation to the sea, so that it is necessary for inland waters to use the table devised for use on land which is given below:

FORCE	DESCRIPTION	SPEED mph	EFFECTS CAUSED
0	Calm	Less than 1	Smoke rises vertically
1	Light Airs	1–3	Smoke shows direction
2	Light Breeze	4–6	Weather vanes moved. Wind felt on face
3	Gentle Breeze	7–10	Wind moves flags. Twigs in constant movement
4	Moderate Breeze	11–16	Dust raised. Small branches in movement
5	Fresh Breeze	17–21	Small trees sway
6	Strong Breeze	22–27	Large branches move
7	Moderate Gale	28–33	Larger trees sway. Walking is difficult
8	Fresh Gale	34–40	Twigs break off. Walking against wind almost impossible

Fig. 68. Beaufort Wind Scale on land

FUEL

The fuel tank should be dipped daily, as part of the over-all engine check which is described in the Appendices to the Manual. It is imperative not to let the fuel tank aboard a power vessel get too low. If a petrol tank is allowed to empty itself, dirt and/or air can get in the fuel line, reducing the engine to a tick-over or stopping it altogether. Running out of diesel fuel is a more serious problem as the injector pump may have to be reprimed, and this is a lengthy job if you have not the right tools and, in any case, it usually requires expert attention.

MOTOR CRUISER EQUIPMENT & FITTINGS

Apart from the marine aspects of boat life and the obvious boat equipment which contributes to the propulsion of your boat through the water, the average cruiser contains a number of other items which contribute to making life more comfortable aboard. How these work and in what ways they may vary from their domestic counterparts on dry land is now described.

THE WATER CLOSET

Make sure that you know how the water closet on board works. On waterways where the authority prohibits the discharge of effluent into the river a chemical closet of the 'Elsan' or 'Racasan' type is usually provided. See that there is an adequate supply of chemical and note the locations of sanitary stations for disposal of the effluent; usually to be found at locks or boatyards.

Sea toilets are a mystery to most people but are not really much more complicated than the domestic type of unit. There are three main patterns of toilet, 1, those that have the pan above the water line, 2, those with the pan level with the water line and 3, those below it. The principle of operation of all three types is much the same. In types 2 and 3 especially, when craft are unattended or at sea the sea-cocks on the inlet and outlet pipes should be closed when not in use. Depending on manufacture the toilet may be provided with one or two operating valves, which are screwed down to close them and unscrewed to open. Usually, the type with one valve has separate pump handles for ejecting effluent (lever type) and filling the pan with sea-water (lift handle). The two-valve type has one pump handle common to both operations, each being carried out independently by opening and closing the requisite valves. When not in use the valve should be closed and a little water left in the bottom of the pan. Before use, the valve control should be

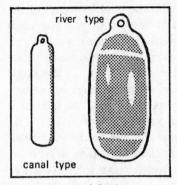

Fig. 64. Types of fender

Fig. 70. Butane gas bottle fixing

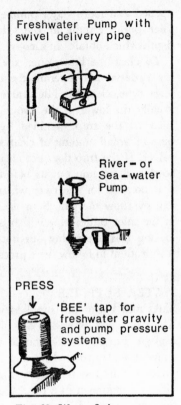

Freshwater Pump with swivel delivery pipe

River – or Sea – water Pump

PRESS

'BEE' tap for freshwater gravity and pump pressure systems

Fig. 69. Water fittings

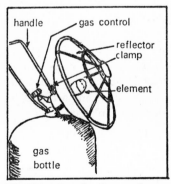

Fig. 71. A safe form of gas heater

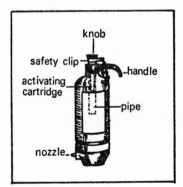

Fig. 72. Modern type fire extinguisher (powder model)

145

opened and more water pumped into the bowl by means of the filler pump handle at the side of the seat to give the usual depth which obtains in a conventional trap. Close the valve.

To clear the bowl, open the valve, usually positioned beside the pedestal and operate the other pump lever (in the single lever type, close the filler valve and open the emptying valve – usually the lower of the two valve controls) until the effluent is clear of the trap, signified by a sucking sound. When clear pump a small amount of clean water into the bowl and close all valves. If the trap does not clear, continue pumping to refill the bowl and repump out as before. Always leave valves closed as it is possible for the river water to back up through the pump and overflow the pan. Some sea-toilets are installed with a loop in the inlet/outlet pipe which is carried up above the waterline to stop this happening but not all are as sophisticated so that it is prudent to follow these precautions.

WATER SUPPLIES

Sinks and basins are supplied with either fresh or river water. The galley sink often has one of each type delivered by separate taps or pumps. A selection of taps are shown in Fig. 69. The conventional washered bib tap can also be used with a variable pressure pump system, since a gravity feed system for water is virtually unknown in a boat. Opening the tap reduces the water pressure in the delivery pipe which automatically switches on an electric pump. As soon as the tap is turned off pressure is applied to the pump switch which promptly isolates the motor. The electric water pump is also provided with a separate switch of its own for safety.

The 'Bee' tap shown in the figure is also a popular type of tap for use with a pressure switch system since the cap is sprung, so that as soon as the cap is released the tap is turned off and water is not accidentally wasted, often an important consideration on smaller craft with small water tank capacities.

GAS APPLIANCES

Besides the gas cooker which is really only a miniature version of the domestic type although a number of large hire cruisers are fitted with a fully fledged domestic model with converted

146

WARNING ! !

'CALOR' or other brands of butane gas, such as 'Gaz' or 'Butagas', are heavier than air and not as strong smelling as coal or natural gas. You are therefore advised to note the following points, especially in relation to the use of the cooker :

1. Always light the match first and hold it to the gas ring before turning on the gas.
2. Do not operate the cooker in draughty conditions.
3. If anything boils over, turn the gas off and only relight it as in 1 above having ensured that no escaped gas is present.
4. If a gas escape is suspected, turn off the bottle and ventilate the boat from stem to stern before using the gas appliances or attempting to start the engine. Since the gas is heavier than air it may sink into the bilges, so that ventilation of this part of your boat should not be overlooked.
5. When not using the cooker turn off the gas supply to the cooker at the gas-cock provided. If no other appliances are served by the gas bottle, turn the bottle valve off by screwing it down. It should be noted that where more than one appliance is served by the gas system, each appliance should have its own gas-cock fitted to the main pipe before its union with any flexible pipe provided.

burners for butane gas, water heaters and refrigerators are also provided on many craft. They work in much the same way as their domestic counterparts but are necessarily equipped with 'fail-safe' devices which make them a little more difficult to light. Water heaters require a permanently lit pilot light to operate and are started by means of turning on the gas supply, placing a lit match to the pilot jet and pressing a bypass button. When lit, remove the match but keep the button pressed down for 10 to 30 seconds. When released, the pilot flame should remain alight. If it does not, repeat the procedure, holding the button down for a longer interval. Some heaters require a full minute before they will remain alight after closure of the bypass valve.

Refrigerators operate in much the same fashion although the method of lighting involves the use of a felt pad, dipped in methylated spirits, which is on the end of a wire handle. The pad is passed to the back of the refrigerator where the gas jet is situated. This is only a matter of convenience owing to the restricted space beneath the unit, the bypass control being positioned at the front of the refrigerator just below the door. Here again, keep the bypass lever or button depressed for 30 seconds or so while the pilot control strip heats up.

ELECTRICITY ABOARD

The normal small cruiser will probably have an electric lighting system and other electrical appliances such as water pump, bilge pump, radio and shaver points. The usual voltage at which these operate is 12 volts D.C., the source of power being supplied by batteries charged by the engine. Separate charging plants are uncommon on small craft owing to their location and weight, but start to appear on craft of 50 feet length and upwards. Sets are finding their way on to the market now which, possibly, will appeal to owners with a little extra cash in their pockets since these are not much bigger than a large suitcase and where perhaps TV and radar equipment is aboard, requiring non-fluctuating higher voltages in alternating current which can be supplied straight from the more sophisticated type of set.

The better equipped dashboard (as at Fig. 9 on page 28) is usually provided with an ammeter, and sometimes a battery state indicator. Some cruisers have automatic voltage regulators as on a car, while others rely on a charging switch being thrown by the ship's engineer to activate the charging circuit until the rate of charge shown on the ammeter has dropped as described on page 27. A normal day's running of five to six hours or even less should keep the battery in a topped up state for the evening use of lights and daily use of the various electrical accessories. If a day ashore is spent and the engine not used it is a wise precaution to run it for an hour or so first thing in the morning, before leaving the cruiser, to ensure that the battery state does not deteriorate, and so that starting difficulties are not experienced on the following day. Running an engine at night for charging purposes is un-neighbourly to say the least.

Wise boat-owners, and a number of charterers too, instal two sets of batteries, one for engine starting and accessories and the other for lighting and power requirements of a more domestic character. Both sets are charged from the engine but drawn on for supplies independently. This ensures that the starter motor on the engine is always supplied by a battery that has not been flattened overnight by more than reasonable use of lighting circuits.

Shaver points are usually provided with a D.C./A.C. inverter of the vibrator type. This delivers an A.C. of 210 to 230 volts of fairly low amperage but sufficient to run a mains voltage electric razor. Insertion of the razor lead plug in the unit's two pin socket starts the vibrator and the razor will start. If you have a 12 volt D.C. tapping on your razor, do not switch to this tapping and use the inverter, but find a suitable outlet supplying 12 volts.

S. Smith and Sons (England) Ltd. import suitable space heating equipment for boats which consists of a blower fan passing air across warm elements and forcing this warmed air along flexible trunking to suitable outlet points on the boat. The equipment can be set to run indefinitely or for limited periods on a clockwork switch which runs back over a preset period to shut off, thus preventing drainage of the battery. The heating element for this type of installation consists of a 'petroil' or paraffin burner, so that an exhaust pipe is fitted to discharge the products of combustion from a hull outlet. Ascertain the location of this outlet when mooring against the bank or quay and other craft as serious damage can be done by the exhaust if not left clear.

HEATERS – NON ELECTRICAL

Gas heaters are also manufactured by the butane gas firms such as 'Calor', 'Butagas' and 'Camping Gaz International'. An adequate heater is shown in the accompanying figure by the latter firm which screws straight into the gas bottle, a method much to be preferred for safety reasons. The same precautions mentioned in connection with gas cookers should always be applied in the case of gas heaters.

Such fires or heaters must be carefully sited if of the portable variety as most are, although it is possible to obtain convector heaters worked by gas or paraffin, which can be fixed to a bulkhead or cabin wall and, ideally, should be provided with a flue.

Paraffin heaters are still very common aboard the small cruiser, even with hire yards. Ensure that these are of the non-spillable variety and store the paraffin well away from the fire itself, preferably in a locker which opens to the outside of the craft.

Any stove which depends on a flame for its heat must have a supply of oxygen. Site the stove, therefore where it can obtain supplies of fresh air for combustion. Do not leave children alone in a cabin where a heater is left on and keep matches etc. well out of their reach. Reflector fires MUST have a safety guard similar to that shown in the illustration which conforms to a British Standard Specification.

Make sure that everyone aboard knows the fire drill which you can evolve from the notes in a following article.

LIGHTING – NON ELECTRICAL

To conserve the batteries, many cruiser owners use butane or paraffin lamps, the latter, best-known, of which is the pressure 'Tilley' lamp. Paraffin is poured into the reservoir and the cap screwed down tightly. The priming lever is then pumped up and down to build up pressure and the lamp lit. As pressure falls the lamp will dim. All that is required is for the priming lever to be pumped again to restore pressure. Non-pressure lamps are easily obtained, the amount of light being controlled by the height of the wick. To douse, it is best to blow across the top of the cover glass, rather than turn the wick down.

Butane gas lamps are also manufactured in a range of patterns and have a light output equivalent to the domestic electric light bulb of 75 watts output. These can be fixed direct to the top of the gas cylinder or mounted on the small cartridges marketed by Camping Gaz International. Running cost is about 7d. per hour. Paraffin costs are somewhat cheaper but with the exception perhaps of the pressure lamp the light output is not as good.

GAS AND PARAFFIN ACCESSORIES SHOULD BE TREATED WITH THE GREATEST RESPECT. ANY EQUIPMENT WHICH IS SUSPECTED NOT TO BE IN FIRST CLASS CONDITION SHOULD NOT BE USED.

FIRE PREVENTION

All craft MUST be provided with fire-fighting equipment and all members of the crew should be shown where it is kept and should acquaint themselves with the methods of operation and disengaging extinguishers etc. from their patent clip, hook, bolt or catch.

In the case of fire, prevention is far better and cheaper than cure. We have already dealt with the rules relative to the gas installation. Make sure plenty of ash-trays are provided for smokers and try to discourage the practices of (a) smoking in bed, and (b) flinging cigarette butts in the river, (if thrown to windward they can, of course, blow back again on to the deck!)

In a general way the use of ordinary chemical extinguishers is to be avoided as there is a possibility of phosgene gas being generated and this, in a confined space, such as the cabin, saloon, wheelhouse or galley of a small boat, can be very dangerous. The type of extinguisher referred to is the C.T.C. type.

For fat fires or those caused by the overheating or accidental usage of electrical equipment, the best type of extinguisher is that providing foam or dry powder since the secret of extinction of any fire is the complete blanketing of the source to eliminate the oxygen in the air necessary to combustion. An asbestos blanket can also be used for this purpose.

The old type of Soda-Acid extinguisher is most effective, since this only squirts out water. The name 'Soda-Acid' is applied to the unit only as a description of the method of working. Soda is added to the water when the extinguisher is filled and a small glass phial of sulphuric acid is inserted in the top of the extinguisher. Striking the knob breaks the phial and a gas formed by the reaction of the acid on the soda forces the water out of the jet nozzle.

Of course, on a boat one of the most useful fire-fighting appliances is a stirrup pump as you should have an ample supply of water. A fine spray nozzle to the delivery hose is recommended for low voltage electrical or fat fires, a method equally as effective as the foam or powder type of extinguisher. In this connection, it should be noted that a foam extinguisher may not produce its foam unless used about fifteen feet away from the fire, so that serious consideration should be given before installing a foam extinguisher anyway. A jet of water should not be used on electrical appliances if still live as the current can run up the jet to the operator if he is at close range.

Sizes of appliances depends on the size of the boat. They should be located at easily accessible points, (a) near the galley, (b) in the wheelhouse, which is often above the engine and close to exit points on to the deck.

Remember, if a fire occurs, NOT to fling all the doors and portholes open but to keep them closed as a fire thrives on fresh air.

TOWING AND USING THE DINGHY

For convenience you may wish to tow a dinghy. On the Broads a dinghy is almost a necessity, where crowded moorings may dictate that you have to moor to an opposite bank to shops, pub or quay.

It is best on an inland waterway to keep the dinghy close on a short painter, towing from the stern of the cruiser. Use a firm cleat or post with a hitch to ensure that it doesn't slip off. When berthing or clearing, detach the dinghy and get a member of the crew to hold the painter while you manoeuvre, telling him to keep the dinghy alongside on the side of the cruiser away from the bank. Whilst under tow, the oars should be brought on board the cruiser or laid along the thwarts of the dinghy with the rowlocks unshipped and their stop strings wound round the oars if there *are* left in the dinghy. Never leave the rowlocks shipped in their sockets when not in use. They can gouge chunks out of topsides if they are!

When leaving the cruiser or parent ship it is correct to embark in the dinghy near the stern. When returning or coming alongside someone else's boat you should board amidships, passing the dinghy to the stern when empty. Don't forget to secure it!! We have heard more funny stories about dinghies lost than any other topic on the river. They may be funny but the many that are founded on fact weren't funny at the time!

TIPS FOR THE HELMSMAN
Remember always to throttle down before changing gear.

Craft with small propellers have little athwartship thrust. Do not rely on it. Use your wheel with forward gear engaged. If you are going too fast – engage reverse. If an unwanted swing starts correct it by a burst AHEAD with the wheel hard over against the swing. Using the helm in reverse is usually frightening!

In wet weather if you have no clear-view screen or wiper, put a line of detergent along the top of the windscreen. This will break up the droplets and give you a better view. When dry again wipe it off carefully as it tends to smear.

SUMMARY

1. Proper care and maintenance of a craft is the basis of a successful cruise. The motor and steering gear should be maintained in good order. Fire fighting appliances should be tested by private owners regularly. Every member of the crew should be instructed in safety drill.
3. A supply of fuel adequate for immediate needs should always be carried, but petrol should never be stowed below deck otherwise than in the craft's fuel tank. Regular checks should be made to guard against leakage of fuel or gas. Naked lights should be extinguished during refuelling.
4. All craft must have proper fenders and all powered craft must have an efficient whistle or hooter.
5 Keep all litter and refuse until you can dispose of it at recognised refuse disposal stations, which are provided at locks, moorings or boatyards. Watch your sewage position carefully and only dispose of it at the proper sewage disposal stations. Sewage should not be disposed of by pumping back into the canal or river. In most cases it is an offence to do so.
6. Users of pleasure craft may be able to help others in an emergency, as well as themselves, if they keep lifebelts and

first-aid equipment handy on their craft.

7. Make sure that the name of your craft and its licence, where applicable is clearly displayed at all times.

WARNING

MAKE SURE WHEN REFUELLING YOUR CRAFT OR TAKING ON WATER THAT YOU ARE USING THE CORRECT FILLER POINT. IF IN DOUBT HAVE A GOOD SNIFF. IF STILL IN DOUBT DIP THE TANK WITH A STICK AND TASTE IT, THE PROCEDURE FOR EXTRACTING WATER FROM FUEL IS COSTLY.
WATER IN THE FUEL WILL KILL THE ENGINE.
FUEL IN THE WATER MAY KILL YOU.

SECTION X

MAN OVERBOARD DRILL
AND FIRST-AID

Man Overboard Drill
Artificial Respiration
Life Jackets
First-aid

Illustrations

F   155

SECTION X

MAN OVERBOARD DRILL AND FIRST-AID

Man Overboard drill on an inland waterway is not quite so complicated as it is at sea. The prime consideration at sea is, of course, not to lose sight of the 'man' or at least manoeuvre your craft so that you can turn and run down the reciprocal of your course, steaming back along your own wake so that you have a fair chance of picking him up. This is often effected by the well-known 'Williamson' turn, which properly done must be calculated from a ship's compass, which an inland cruiser rarely possesses.

The basic rules, however, apply in that the action of the helmsman must be FAST and that the crew member spotting the accident should holler 'MAN OVERBOARD – PORT!' or 'MAN OVERBOARD – STARBOARD!' as the case may be. The helmsman should put the wheel in the direction called. This is designed to kick the stern clear of the man in the water. If there is time a lifebelt should be flung towards the 'man' to assist him keeping afloat, since even a strong swimmer can be severely hampered if fully clothed. The turn should be continued in the same direction by backing and filling, and the craft brought to the position of the 'man', with him fine on the port or starboard bow, having regard to wind and propeller effects. Make sure that your bow will not sheer away from him at the crucial moment just prior to picking him up. Use a rope with a bowline on the end which provides a generous loop for getting him aboard.

If proceeding upstream, it may be necessary when returning downstream for a man to pass him and turn again, as trying to heave a man aboard when travelling with the current is fraught with difficulties, especially if you are trying to take way off by running the engine in reverse. You may run him down or miss him altogether. From tests we have made on the Thames we have found it far quicker to adopt this method, i.e. always passing and turning to face upstream before attempting to pick the man up.

Never try to stop the cruiser and drift back to the 'man'. Remember that he is probably drifting as fast as you are.

If *you* fall overboard, swim for the bank or even try touching the bottom. If you are on a canal you will probably find you can wade ashore!

THIS KIND OF ACCIDENT IS NOT AS UNCOMMON AS YOU MIGHT SUPPOSE. NON-SWIMMERS SHOULD BE ENCOURAGED TO WEAR LIFE-JACKETS AT ALL TIMES, AND SHOULD NOT BE REQUESTED TO TAKE ON RISKY EXERCISE AT LOCKS AND MOORINGS.

NOTE

Owners of craft will be aware that it is very difficult to get a man aboard in mid-stream from out of the water owing to the increased weight of wet clothing. If possible, it is strongly recommended that some form of collapsible ladder or step notches be provided so that a foothold can be obtained below the water-line. Step-notches can be provided in the transom.

It should be emphasised that no incident of this nature should ever be treated lightly. Serious consequences have been known where the crew of a cruiser have assumed that someone who has fallen in can take care of himself. Neither should it be assumed that a known strong swimmer is able to keep afloat under such circumstances. On the crew member's rescue it may be necessary to revive him and the notes given below should be carefully followed if artificial respiration is deemed to be required. It should be given as soon as possible as the time lag between falling in and becoming asphyxiated is very short indeed, in some cases as little as three to four minutes.

METHOD

1. Lay the patient on his back and, if on a slope, have the stomach slightly lower than the chest. Make a brief inspection of the mouth and throat to ensure that they are clear of obvious obstructions. Give the patient's head the maximum backwards tilt as shown by the arrows in Fig. 73, Plate 'A', so that the chin is prominent, the mouth closed and the neck stretched to give a clear airway.

2. Open your mouth wide, make an airtight seal over the nose of the patient and blow. The operator's cheek or the hand

157

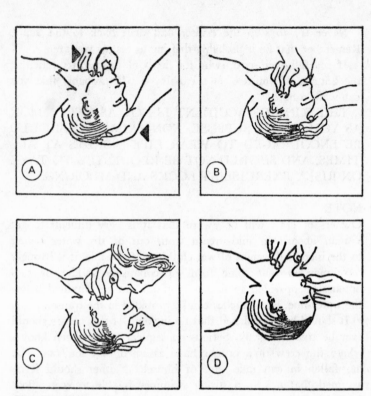

Figs. 73 and 74

supporting the chin can be used to seal the patient's lips as shown in Plate 'B'.

3. If the nose is blocked, open the patient's mouth using the hand supporting the chin, open your mouth wide and make an airtight seal over his mouth and blow as in Plate 'C'. This may also be used as an alternative to the mouth-to-nose technique even when the nose is not blocked, in which case the nostrils must be sealed with the fingers as shown in Plate 'D'. The wrist must be kept low on the patient's forehead to ensure that the full tilt of the head is maintained.

If the patient's mouth cannot be opened, blow through his parted lips as the air passing between his teeth may be sufficient to inflate his lungs. After exhaling, turn your head to watch for chest movement whilst inhaling deeply ready for blowing again.

If the chest does not rise, check that the patient's mouth and throat are free of obstruction and the head is tilted as far back as possible. Blow again. If air enters the patient's stomach through blowing too hard, press the stomach gently, with the head of the patient turned to one side.

Commence with four quick inflations of the patient's chest to give rapid build-up of oxygen in the patient's blood and then slow down to to twelve to fifteen respirations per minute or blow again each time the patient's chest has deflated.

With small children and babies, inflation at the rate of twenty per minute is achieved by a series of puffs, each one ceasing as the chest starts to rise.

UNDER NO CIRCUMSTANCES BLOW VIOLENTLY INTO A BABY'S LUNGS.

Before resuscitation, breathe deeply with the mouth open to build up the oxygen content.*

LIFE JACKETS

The wearing of proper life-jackets cannot be too heavily stressed, although it is admitted that on inland waters their necessity is doubted by many. However, children should be encouraged to wear them, and many feel considerably more dressed for the part when they have got them on. We have never found any difficulty in persuading children to accept them as part of their boating dress.

Many firms market a type of jacket which is referred to as a 'personal buoyancy aid' but it should be noted that these are not as effective as the proper 'life-jacket'. A life-jacket for an adult should have a minimum buoyancy of 30 lbs. and be capable of bring the wearing into the 'riding' position within 3 to 5 seconds. A British Standard exists for life-jackets and you should only therefore buy a brand which conforms to this standard (B.S. No. 3595 :63). Some are inflated by mouth, others by CO_2 cartridges, which are built into the jacket while others possess both methods of inflation, the latter being available as an emergency precaution if the wearer does fall in and is thereby prevented from inflating the jacket himself.

* Based on notes by the British Safety Council and Royal Life Saving Society.

Cruiser hire firms normally supply adequate 'life-jackets' either free on request or for a nominal charge or deposit. It is safer to ask for them than wait to be asked.

FIRST AID
Always carry a first aid kit with you when you cruise. The types of kit sold for motorists are probably the handiest but if you are holidaying in hot weather and/or out of this country make extra provision for sun-burn (such as calamine lotion) and change of diet if you are to buy your food locally. Investment in a handy bottle of good quality disinfectant is strongly recommended, as well.

APPENDICES

A. Engine and Boat Maintenance
B. Suggested Tool Kit List
C. The Norfolk and Suffolk Broads
D. Inland Waterways Overseas (Europe)
E. Books, Charts and Maps

Illustrations

161

APPENDIX 'A'

ENGINE AND BOAT MAINTENANCE

THE ENGINE

Whether your engine is a petrol or diesel engine the following points apply. If you are hiring your cruiser from a competent boat yard, they will show you what daily maintenance they require and this is covered in the foregoing list. However, if your craft is your own or you have hired it from a private individual whose attention to maintenance you have reason to doubt it is as well to follow the suggestions which follow and which are found in most marine engine manufacturers' handbooks.

COOLING SYSTEMS

If a 'keel cooler' is incorporated in the engine installation, there will be a header tank which must be topped up with fresh water daily. Engine cooling only is dealt with by this system in recent models, but earlier models, especially of the B.M.C. range were also provided with exhaust jackets which were supplied from the closed circuit, so that water would not be expelled from the exhaust system as in the open type of cooling system which takes sea- or river-water inboard to cool the engine and discharges it through the exhaust by way of a mixing chamber. Alternatively, recent B.M.C. models are provided with a separate exhaust cooling system which does use the sea- or river-water which is operated by a gear driven water pump from the engine. Thus one finds two cooling systems applicable to the engine, one for the cylinder block (closed circuit with keel cooler) and one for the exhaust (sea-water circuit through strainer to pump and thence via the mixing chamber out through the exhaust pipe).

It is therefore imperative not to ignore the sea-water filter, if you are told that the craft possesses a 'keel cooler', since the presence of such does not necessarily imply that there is no sea-water circuit.

LUBRICATION

The matter of lubrication cannot be stressed too much. You may decide to inspect the engine sump dipstick daily and ignore the gear dip-sticks, of which there may be more than one! This applies mainly to craft having reduction gearing. Do not forget a weekly check on lubrication of throttle and gear linkages on the controls, topping up of battery and if reduction gear is fitted give the coupling flange greaser a turn. Examine all fuel lines and oil lines and junctions for leaks and on diesel engines the surplus oil should be drained from the injection pump camshaft chamber where instructed by the manufacturer.

MAINTENANCE

After 150 hours which represents about three weeks continuous day-time running the basic service should be carried out on the engine which consists of changing the engine oil, renewing the oil and fuel filters and cleaning the air cleaner element. Add a drop or two of oil to the dynamo lubricator and check the tension, adjusting as described at No. 16 on page 167. It is not unwise to check the tightness of all bolts, not only on the engine installation but also on the steering gear at this time.

Recently, many craft have started to be fitted with a transverse-mounted engine in the stern which drives a hydraulic motor, which, in turn, drives the propeller. In these cases, no stern tube greaser will be located, but it is important to check the level of the reservoir containing the hydraulic oil, which is of a special grade.

Oil cannot be drained from the sump in a boat in the same way as from a road vehicle, since the drain plug is usually completely inaccessible. A pump is therefore usually mounted on the after section of the engine and can also be utilised by means of a tee union below the pump cylinder for emptying the gear-box as well. To drain the engine open the cock in the pipe leading to the pump from the engine sump, open the pump rod retaining cap and pour a little engine oil into the cylinder. This will help to prime the pump. Screw the cap down tightly and holding a bucket or can under the outlet pipe pump firmly until the sump is empty, denoted by a considerable sucking sound and a miserable drip of oil from the outlet. This operation is eased considerably by removing the oil filler cap from the rocker cover or other location which such might have. DO NOT FOR-GET TO CLOSE THE SUMP PIPE COCK. Failure to do so will interfere with the correct build up of oil pressure when the engine is filled and re-started.

Gear-box oil change is usually only necessary at every other 150 service (i.e. every 300 hours or six weeks).

FUEL CARE

It is most important in the case of both petrol and diesel engines to make sure that fuel is clean and that all lines are leak-proof and that there is plenty of fuel available to the engine. Air locks in petrol lines are a nuisance, to say the least, but in diesel lines can be even more troublesome. Dirt in petrol can block a jet in the carburetter, which, if the cause be found is easy to clean and replace. Dirt in diesel fuel, may be easy to diagnose but involves a lengthy and tricky operation to cure and restore to normal running.

BATTERIES

Do not ignore your batteries. Inspect them frequently. Keep them clean and dry and check that the terminals are tight and free of the crystalline deposits which frequently form. If a battery shows signs of failing to hold its charge, it probably needs replacing. If you cannot get hold of a replacement immediately do not leave it aboard connected up when you leave the boat, but bring it ashore and try trickle charging it occasionally until you have to use it again, with a 'low rate charge'. Do not have it 'booster charged' or continuously charged by a garage as this will be detrimental and destroy any further life that it might have.

GAS CYLINDERS

To ascertain if a gas cylinder is empty, it should be borne in mind that a full gas cylinder weighs considerably more than an empty one, since the gas is stored in liquid form. This latter fact can also be used for testing the content of a cylinder if you have not a full one to use as a comparison by weight. Rocking of the cylinder or tapping the side will usually give an indica-tion of its contents. The priming lever referred to on page 165 is a fitment usually found on Continental craft, since British pattern regulators supplied for use with 'Calor' gas are automatic in operation.

Reference should be made to the chart on page 166. The chart shows all usual maintenance items required to the working parts of a cruiser. The double ringed items are those requiring daily attention, whilst those in the single rings require attention at less frequent intervals or only when circumstances dictate, as follows :

DAILY
1. Check the engine oil level by means of the dipstick.
2. Top up with recommended grade of oil through filler. Replace filler cap tightly.
3. Check gear-box oil level and top up if necessary. Gear-box dipsticks are usually built into the filler cap.
4. Turn the sterntube greaser until resistance is felt.
5. (Only if operating in weedy conditions.) Close seacocks, if any, remove and clean strainers. Replace carefully and turn caps down tight. OPEN SEA-COCKS. This operation should also be carried out if you suspect a blockage or have gone aground.
6. Where the engine has a freshwater primary circuit top up the header tank with fresh water.
7. Turn off the gas cock when cooker not in use. If the cooker is the only gas appliance aboard, turn off at the Gas Cylinder (9).
8. Where a hand-operated bilge pump is provided, pump out the bilges every morning. Electric bilge pumps should not be forgotten, either. Switch them on when you first get under way. Some are driven direct off the engine so do not need attention.

PERIODICALLY
9. Always turn off the gas bottle when changing cylinders. If a regulator is provided, pump the knob up and down to prime it. (Continental models only.)
10. Every two or three days dip the water tank either with the dipstick provided or through the filler pipe. Top up.
11. Fill until water enters the stand-pipe. Screw cap down.

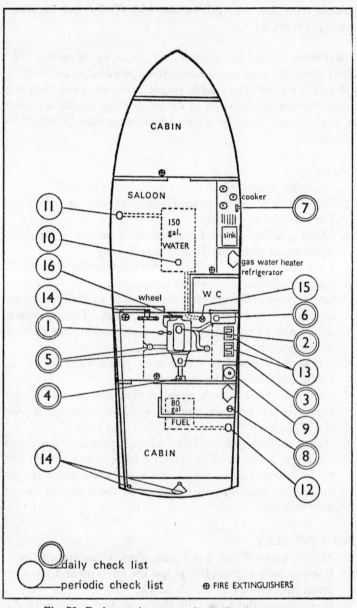

Fig. 75. Cruiser maintenance chart. (See following text
for explanation of symbols)

12. Watch your fuel gauge or dip the tank regularly. On petrol boats with small capacities it may be wise to do this daily. When filling make sure the gas cooker is not in use and forbid smoking in the area. Strain the fuel through a straining funnel if you can.
13. Weekly. Top up the batteries with distilled water.
14. Occasionally see that the steering cables and linkages are not dry. If necessary apply graphite grease.
15. If the freshwater supply runs out, draining the tank, it may be necessary to reprime the pump. This is done by locating the priming cock, opening it and pouring a little water into the funnel above it. When the funnel fills, close the cock and test by operating one of the taps.
16. If the engine fails to charge the batteries, check the tightness of the pulley belt round the dynamo. If slack loosen the bolts holding the dynamo and swing it away from the engine. Retighten the bolts.

APPENDIX 'B'

SUGGESTED TOOL KIT LIST
Marlin Spike
1 lb. hammer
2 lb. hammer
Saw set (Tenon, Hack, Long, Keyhole, Rip) and handle
Pliers
Pipe wrench
'Mole' grip
Stilsons
Tin cutter $2\frac{1}{2}$ in.
Set of 4 screwdrivers
Rasp
Flat files (2)
Whitworth Socket set with ratchet arm and 10 in. extension bar
A-F Socket set for use with above
Rotary Hand-drill $\frac{1}{4}$ in. chuck
Set of drill bits up to $\frac{1}{4}$ in.
Carpenter's Brace
Set of brace bits and countersinker
Plug spanner

Feeler gauges
Adjustable spanner (large)
Ditto (small)
Vice 2½ in – 3 in.
Set of Whitworth and A-F open ended spanners
(Ditto ring spanners if preferred)
Grease gun
Carpenter's Square
Oil can
Wire stripper
Valve compressor clamp
Philips screwdriver
Glass cutter
Pin punch
Flat scraper
OBA, 1BA, 2BA & 3BA small spanners
Two chisels

MATERIALS

Grinding Paste, Grease, Oil, Tube of Evo-Stick Adhesive, Wood Filler, 'Pluggit', Insulating Tape.

Screws, Nails, Panel Pins, Staples and a selection of Whitworth bolts, nuts and washers in useful sizes.

The above list is not completely exhaustive but represents a tool kit collected by one of the authors over a number of years and has been found sufficient to tackle most carpentry, electrical and engine overhaul jobs that might be found on a boat.

APPENDIX 'C'

THE NORFOLK AND SUFFOLK BROADS

The Norfolk and Suffolk Broads are interconnected lakes, formed over the centuries from old peat workings, the main linking rivers being the Yare, Bure and Waveney, all of which are tidal and enter the sea at Great Yarmouth. Oulton Broad which is connected to the Waveney by a short canal can also be entered from Lowestoft through Mutford Lock. Numerous motor cruiser charter firms operate on the Broads which has become the most popular motor yachting centre in the country. Sailing craft, once the most popular type of boat are rapidly disappearing and motor craft now outnumber the familiar Broads sailer by an appreciable amount.

Since the whole system is tidal a certain amount of care is necessary in navigating, especially in the environs of Great Yarmouth, i.e. across Breydon Water, where a channel is marked by piles and for a distance of approximately six miles up the three main rivers. The tidal variations at the upper limits of navigation are minimal, being about 3 inches to six inches.

The River Yare, from Norwich to Yarmouth has a certain amount of commercial traffic, in the shape of colliers and small coastal cargo vessels, which should be treated with a certain amount of caution. (See pages 7 and 8.) Swing bridges on the Yare are only operated for these vessels. Small craft must lower their masts and wheelhouse roofs where necessary to negotiate these bridges.

CAUTION

It should be noted that due to the restricted exit of the River Bure at Yarmouth, this river continues to flow after the tide has turned to the ebb in Breydon Water. Craft proceeding from Breydon Water into the Bure should therefore try to arrange to pass from Breydon Water into the mouth of the Bure about an hour *before* High Water. In the other direction, try to arrive at the mouth of the Bure at slack water on a low tide so that the rising tide in Breydon water will assist you upstream on the Yare or the Waveney.

If you get into the Bure and find the tide still against you it is best to tie up at the Yarmouth Yacht Station which is on the right bank as you proceed upstream about 3 furlongs above the mouth of the river. When turning into the river keep close to the marker posts on your left.

AUTHORITY

The Broads are under the control and general superintendence of the Great Yarmouth Port and Haven Commissioners, 21, South Quay, Great Yarmouth, (Tel: 4547) although they are not in all cases the owning body. Private owners wishing to enter the Broads or place craft thereon from trailers, should apply to the above for all necessary details of registration and licence fees etc. Oulton Broad and Dyke are dealt with by the Oulton Broad Joint Committee, Lowestoft.

APPENDIX 'D'

INLAND WATERWAYS OVERSEAS (EUROPE)

The Continental inland waterways are an extensive network, basically linking the River Rhine with the Seine and the Seine with the Rhône. Thus, not only is it possible for traffic to pass from Switzerland and Germany through the Netherlands to France by water, but also from the English Channel to the Mediterranean, without the long sea-voyage round Spain and through the Strait of Gibraltar. Further, small craft can enter the Bay of Biscay from the southernmost part of the network by using the famous Canal du Midi and joining the lateral canal of the Garonne river at Toulouse to Bordeaux.

1. FRANCE

Canal building on the Continent was contemporary with that in the British Isles, perhaps a little earlier and it must be admitted that the French were experts at it, for example their famous canal engineer Ferdinand de Lesseps was responsible for the building of the Suez Canal and had planned a canal through the isthmus of Panama many years before it came to be built. In fact they are still building canals, being aware of the advantages of water transport of bulk cargoes. All the waterways are state owned and have been for many years.

One will appreciate, therefore, that these waterways are very much in commercial use, the barges, 'péniches' being a familiar sight or obstacle to the pleasure boat on the main routes. These are the Rivers Marne, Seine, Yonne, Sâone and Rhône and the Canal de Bourgogne, besides certain lateral canals which were built alongside unnavigable rivers. The presence of considerable commercial traffic, however, has one advantage, for, at the time of writing, pleasure craft pay no toll or licence fee for use of the waterways apart from the documentary formalities of a 'Permis de Navigation', which is the ship's log book or registration certificate, a 'Permis de Circulation' being the Chief Engineer's permit to use the canals and, for certain waterways, a pilot's licence or 'Certificat de Capacité'.

All locks are manned by keepers and boat crews are discouraged from working locks for themselves although their assistance is often welcomed, especially in remote regions where the lock-keeper may be a pensioner or widow or even a housewife whose husband, the official lock-keeper, is tending the orchard or the cattle which he finds more lucrative in view of the minimal traffic on the canal. Tipping the lock-keeper is appreciated especially on the commercial routes, but from our own experience on lesser frequented waterways such as the Canal du Nivernais these people are often overjoyed at being given something to do.

There are two hire firms in France, chartering a range of motor cruisers for inland use, the oldest being Peter Zivy's Société Anonyme Internationale de Navigation Touristique or S.A.I.N.T. Line of 77,-Poincy par Trilport, Seine-et-Marne, France, who operate some ten cruisers from two bases, one at Poincy, which is about thirty miles from Paris up the River Marne and the other at Baye, forty miles south of Auxerre on the summit level of the Canal du Nivernais. The younger firm which commenced business at Toulouse in 1969 is a subsidiary of Blue Line Cruisers Ltd., a British firm of; The Boatyard, Braunston, Near Rugby, England.

Before entering France with your own boat, you should enquire for full details of the formalities from the French Tourist Office, at 178, Piccadilly, London, W.1. or from the S.A.I.N.T. Line at the address given above.

The general rules concerning the 'rule of the river' having

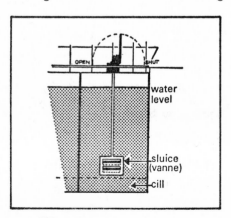

Fig. 76. French sluices operate by the 'hit and miss' principle

international recognition generally apply. For complete listings of the canals and diagrams there is an excellent French publication entitled 'Guide de la Navigation Interieure' which is published in two volumes and can be obtained through the French Tourist Office or from Capt. O. M. Watts, Ltd. of 49, Albemarle Street, London, S.W.1. Excellent strip maps of the more important rivers published in France are obtainable, again from S.A.I.N.T. Line Cruisers who, incidentally, exhibit every year at the International Boat Show in London.

SIGNS AND SIGNALS

Signs and lights in red denote obstructed or prohibited passage and appear at channel entrances, over bridge arches, etc. Orange or amber denotes caution due to an obstruction or restricted channel. White or green denote that the channel is clear. These follow recently adopted rules and may not apply everywhere. Adaptations of International Road Signs are quite common especially with regard to mooring and speed restrictions, bridge headrooms and channel widths etc.

At entrances to some tunnels and the larger commercial locks on the Seine, Yonne, and Rhône lateral canal system, traffic lights are often employed. 'Red' denotes that the lock or tunnel is in use and you should stop and keep clear of the entrance. 'Red' and 'Green' together or 'Amber' denote that you may prepare to move in and 'Green' that the passage is clear. Fig. 77 gives some common examples of some of the signs that may be met.

SOUND SIGNALS

There is a comprehensive set of sound signals recognised on Continental Waterways, both in France and the Netherlands which is shown below :

Turning to Port — —

Turning to Starboard —

Leaving a Berth ——

Stopping —— ——

Mooring (in fog) —— 15 sec. intervals

I wish to overtake
to Port —— — —
to Starboard —— —
You may overtake
to Port — —
to Starboard —
You may not
overtake — — — —

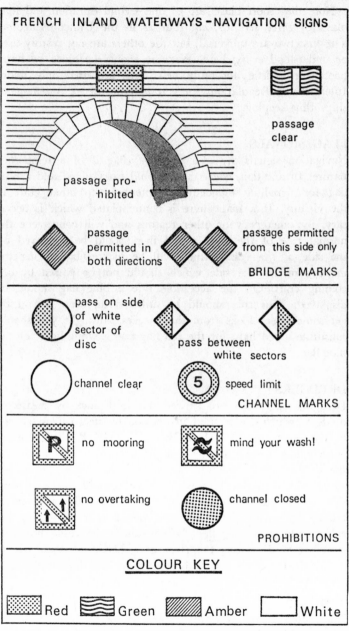

Fig. 77

Note that short blasts are of one second duration and long blasts of *three* seconds, *not* four as in the United Kingdom. The first two are universal, but the others are not readily used or understood everywhere. Warning should be given by horn, hooter or whistle *not* on a bell. Bells are used only under International Regulations for certain types of fog warning, or ships' time-keeping.

FLAG SIGNALS

Navigation signals are also given by flag if of a temporary nature. In addition, every craft should carry a red and a blue flag for signalling manoeuvring intentions to other craft in the vicinity. If a manoeuvre is contemplated which is necessary, for emergency or other reasons and will contravene the normal rule of the river a red flag should be displayed on the side of the vessel which will be inaccessible during the manoeuvre, i.e. the side which should not be passed by oncoming craft. On the accessible side a blue flag should be displayed. This rule should be adhered to, even if you do get some queer looks from the bargees. At night you should substitute a red light for the red flag and a white light for the blue flag.

DREDGERS

Dredging operations are carried out in France by means of dredgers which are secured in position by steel cables secured to the banks on BOTH SIDES OF THE RIVER. Vessels approaching a dredger should be prepared to stop and wait for the dredger crew to lower the cable across the wider chanel, which will be marked by a white disc, displayed on the relevant side of the dredger. Proceed as soon as the cable is lowered, taking the centre of the channel offered to avoid fouling the cable with your propeller. When raised, the cable normally stretches tautly across the river at a height of about six to eight feet. It is therefore inadvisable to try and shoot under it.

2. HOLLAND

The Dutch inland waterways system is one that has developed with considerable technical ease to some extent due to the level terrain of the country. One can motor for many miles without coming upon a lock. It is perhaps true to say that for the pure *boating* enthusiast, Holland does not offer as much variety as the United Kingdom, Eire or France, but a number of firms offer cruising facilities in hire craft, details of which can be obtained from the Dutch National Tourist Office A.N.V.V., 38, Hyde Park Gate, London, S.W.7. – Telephone number 01–584 6781. Private owners wishing to enter Dutch inland waters should also apply to the same office for details of navigation regulations and formalities. See also 'Inland Waterways of Holland' (published Imray Laurie and Wilson) 45s.

3. IRISH FREE STATE (EIRE)

The main waterway on which excellent cruising facilities exist is the River Shannon. The river is navigable for over 140 miles and is suitable for the average river cruiser between Killaloe and a point well above Carrick-on-Shannon. The estuary, for sea-going craft entering the Shannon can be very tricky up as far as Killaloe, so that detailed study of local charts and instructions which can be obtained from the Shannon Navigation Offices should be made, at their offices at Limerick or Athlone. A pilot is available off Scattery Island for the inward passage to Limerick.

The river contains a number of Loughs, the two biggest being Lough Ree and Lough Derg, navigating through which should be only attempted if a hand-bearing compass and good binoculars are carried. Quite steep seas can be encountered on these in windy weather. Hire craft owners renting from yards on the Shannon advise their clients not to attempt a passage in such conditions. Details of the navigation marks used on the Shannon are shown in the accompanying Plate, (Fig. 78). Further information on cruiser hire or formalities for the private owner wishing to enter Eire are obtainable from the Irish Tourist Office, Ireland House, 150, New Bond Street, London, W.1. – Telephone number 01–493 3201, or from the Board of Public Works, 51, St Stephen's Green, Dublin, in respect of the latter.

4. GERMANY

The River Rhine is the main arterial waterway of Europe, carrying large commerical ships, the familiar Rhine barge and

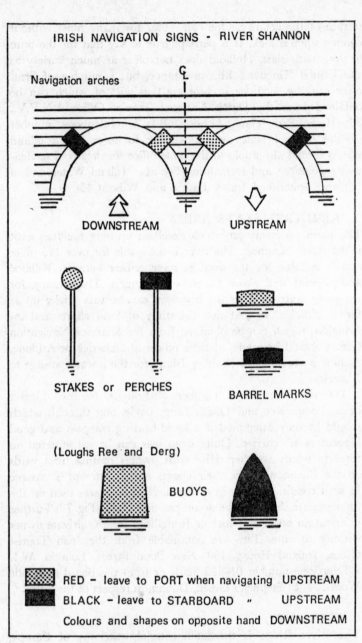

Fig. 78. Shannon River marks

176

a number of tourist passenger boats. Inland waterway cruiser hire as we understand it is not prevalent in view of the essential commercial nature of the waterway. Canals link the Rhine through Holland and Belgium with France.

Private owners wishing to enter the Rhine should enquire for all details from the German Tourist Information Bureau, 61, Conduit Street, London, W.1. – Telephone number 01–734 2600, or the Dutch National Tourist Office A.N.V.V. as above.

5. BELGIUM

Similar comments apply in Belgium to those made in respect of Holland. The waterways are mainly commercial, comprising linking routes from the Rhine and Dutch ports into the North East of France. For detailed study of the Navigation facilities available there is an excellent volume by E. E. Benest, 'The Inland Waterways of Belgium' (published by Imray, Laurie and Wilson) 45s.

APPENDIX 'E'

1. BOOKS ON HANDLING, PILOTAGE ETC.

Little Ship Handling: Motor Vessels by Lt. Cmdr. M. J. Rantzen, R.N.V.R. (Herbert Jenkins – 1966)

Boat World (Annually by Business Dictionaries Ltd.)

Launch Digest (Thames Conservancy – Annually)

Thames Navigation and General Bye-Laws, 1957 (Thames Conservancy)

The Maintenance of Inboard Engines by E. Delmar-Morgan (Newnes)

Saint Line Cruisers: Instruction Manual. (Revised periodically) (S.A.I.N.T. Line, Poincy par Trilport, France)

Teach Yourself Motor Boating by Noble and Shimmin (E.U.P.)

Port of London Authority Bye-Laws (Port of London Authority – 1968)

National Motor Launch and Powerboat Certificate syllabus (R.Y.A.)

British Waterways Board General Canal Bye-Laws, (1965)

Anchors and Moorings by Lt. Cmdr. A. Colin (Maritime Press)

Small Craft Engines and Equipment by E. Delmar Morgan (Adlard Coles)

177

Outboard Motors by Hans Mermanson (Adlard Coles – 1970)

Handyman Afloat and Ashore by Ken Bramham (Adlard Coles – 1970)

2. GENERAL INTEREST

Holiday Cruising on Inland Waterways by Charles Hadfield & Michael Streat (David and Charles)

Waterways Holiday Guide (Inland Waterways Association – Annually)

New Waterways (I.W.A.)

Canals and Waterways, A Brief Guide by Charles Hadfield (Raleigh)

The Watney Book of Inland Waterways by Viscount St Davids (Queen Anne Press)

The Inland Waterways Association also stock a large selection of books on the history of canals and other titles of fiction and non-fiction concerning the waterways.

3. CHARTS AND MAPS covering the entire Inland Waterways system of England and Wales are obtainable from :

Inland Waterways Association,
114 Regents Park Road,
London, N.W.1.

British Waterways Board,
Melbury House,
Melbury Terrace,
London, N.W.1.

Edward Stanford Ltd.,
12–14 Long Acre,
London, W.C.2.

Imray Laurie & Wilson,
Wych House,
St Ives,
Huntingdon.

or most chart agents or marine shops.

Information about canals in Scotland may be obtained from the following :

Caledonian Canal :
Manager and Engineer,
Caledonian Canal Office,
Clachnaharry,
Inverness.

Crinan Canal :
Engineer-in-Charge,
Old Basin Works,
Applecross Street,
Glasgow, C.4.

Index